The Story
World's Favorite

THE CANADIAN BRASS BOOK

By Rick Walters

HLP Hal Leonard Publishing Corporation

7777 West Bluemound Road P O Box 13819 Milwaukee WI 53213

Exclusively Distributed by

Hal Leonard Publishing Corporation
7777 West Bluemound Road
P.O. Box 13819
Milwaukee, WI 53213

First printing: August 1992

ISBN 0-79351-665-X

CONTENTS

ACKNOWLEDGMENTS

Many people have been most gracious in their assistance to me in writing this book. I am grateful for the excellent and extensive preparatory research accomplished by Virginia Saya and her assistant, Maria Virobik. Phyllis Ohanian, and especially Laura Kohrs were very helpful proofreaders. Costa Pilavachi made many comments that were very helpful to me. As is so often the case, I am indebted to Steve Rauch for his patience with me. Many people made their photos available for inclusion in the book, particularly Fred Mills from his vast collection, along with all the other members of the Canadian Brass, and also Kevin Watts, Keith Watts, Walt Baranger, and others. Most of all I would like to thank Chuck, Gene, Fred, Ron, and David for their generous participation in bringing their story to the page.

WHO *ARE* THESE GUYS?

The scene: an airport somewhere in North America. Five men come off a flight and head down the crowded concourse to the main terminal, with the Pachelbel Canon sounding over the speakers. One stops to buy a newspaper, one heads to the john, and one stops to make a quick call on a pay phone. The other two do nothing worth mentioning. Well, O.K.—if you must know, one buys a lottery ticket while the other tells him not to. As they regroup, heading toward the baggage claim area, they notice a sizable crowd of people gathering around them. Accustomed to the limelight, the five casually pass the time, trying not to notice the commotion that is beginning. Though distracted with thoughts of their celebrity, they chat about where to have lunch, when rehearsals will begin, and just exactly what city they're in. The crowd pushes closer, brushing up against the men. One feels a strong tug on his sleeve, and as casually as possible mentions that perhaps they should consider looking for security guards to help them get through the adoring mob. A young woman in a tight red dress begins screaming, "It's them! It's them!" Reporters and TV cameras hit the scene. Just then, in what seems like a reprieve from the danger that fame can bring, the five men spot their bags and head toward them, each one grumbling about the lack of privacy (but not exactly displeased with the attention of dozens of ripe young women pressing closer and closer). The crowd loses control. Three girls dressed in tight bright spandex jump onto the baggage carousel and start making an eager climb over. Fear and terror (mixed with flattery and delight) flash through the five pairs of eyes. Seeing no way out, they huddle down together, praying that some sign of rationality and reason will prevail among the feverish fans. Body smashes against body. The sound of clothes ripping pierces the air. Screams—like Beatlemania. The flash of cameras. Fame can be such a rough and dirty game. Like rugby.

Then suddenly, the huddled group of five realizes that the crowd has... has *passed them by*, and is tearing the clothes off some other guys down the way, for goodness sake! Awkward silence as they avert their eyes from one another. One fumbles for his glasses and starts to make out the banners: U2 WE LOVE YOU. With faces as red as a Canadian maple leaf, another starts to look for change for the luggage cart machine. Without incident, within minutes every bag, trombone and tuba is out on the curb at the cab stand.

The cabbie looks surprised. "What is all this stuff, anyway?"
"Horns, trumpets, trombones and like that."
"You guys got some kind of act or somethin'?"
"Yeah, we're the Canadian Brass."
"I thought you might be with those rock stars comin' in today."
"Uh... no."

It's just another wacky day in show-biz.

B E G I N N I N G S

Just how did the most successful chamber ensemble in history get started? As is usual with most worthwhile endeavors, the Canadian Brass took a few years to get off the ground. A key ingredient was that each of the members had played in brass quintets before coming together, and each had an enthusiasm and love for playing brass chamber music. It also didn't hurt that they happened to be multi-talented individuals with a hurricane of collective creative energy. They were all natural born hams. And, oh yes, did we forget to mention that they can play the horns better than just about anybody around?

In 1970, playing in a brass quintet was not exactly the most likely way to make a living in music. Apart from the Philip Jones Ensemble in England, there had never before been a professional, full-time, classically oriented brass group, and certainly never a brass quintet. At that time the only model was the New York Brass Quintet, but even the players in that excellent pioneering ensemble did not receive their principal income from their concertizing. Certainly no brass quintet had toured the world, appeared regularly on television, or had a major recording career. After all, brass quintets by modern definition had only existed since about 1950. In the 1950s and 1960s many committed brass players had formed quintets primarily for their own enjoyment, but at that time anyone who believed that it could be a full-time career would have been considered a deluded nut. Gene Watts was just nuts enough to believe that it was possible.

Two members of the Canadian Brass had actually played together in a quintet at least two years before any plans were firmly laid for a professional ensemble. Gene and Fred Mills were both playing at the Shakespeare Festival in the summer of 1968 in Stratford, Ontario. They pulled in some other players, and sat around the basement of the theatre playing through quintet arrangements for pure pleasure. That was it for the time being. Gene tried to put together a brass quintet over the next couple of years, but as he describes it, it was always "the revolving door plan" —players coming and going.

Gene had moved to Toronto in 1966 to play trombone in the Toronto Symphony under conductor Seiji Ozawa. By the time he left the orchestra in 1970, it was clear to him that what he wanted most in life was *not* to play in a symphony orchestra. He had the idea to form a professional brass quintet. Gene had spent a good deal of time becoming a regular in the free-lance scene in Toronto, and believed that somehow his connections would lead the way in forming the group. At just about the time he began the pursuit, Chuck Daellenbach moved to Canada to begin a teaching position at the University of Toronto. The two met right away. If there was any one event that sparked the launching of the group, it was this meeting and almost instant partnership of Chuck and Gene. Chuck recalls:

> I had a briefcase full of brass music. I quite innocently said, 'Why don't we play through some quintets?' I had no idea he had been eating and sleeping brass quintets for three years. He was very sly. I also had no idea that he was actually auditioning me. As we began to talk about the possibilities for a professional quintet, I saw immediately in my unmistakable wisdom that this fellow *might* be some sort of genius with some revolutionary and yet reasonable ideas, and that his crazy ideas combined with my tendencies toward over-achievement might lead to something more than interesting.

They discovered that they had both been devoted students of Arnold Jacobs, and had practically everything else in common as well.

One of the first things they did was to call Gene's old buddy, Fred. Fred was living in Ottawa, playing with the National Arts Centre Orchestra. While the idea of playing in a brass quintet was interesting to him, he decided that for the time being he'd prefer to stay in Ottawa with a well-paid position, with full government benefits, playing first trumpet in a top-flight orchestra, rather than join a couple of guys in Toronto in their cooked-up scheme. (Who could blame him?) After various trial combinations, Gene at last

5

Early 1970s; streetcorners, taverns—anywhere people will listen.

Caricature from the 1970s.

assembled the first true edition of the Canadian Brass Ensemble (as it was called at the time), consisting of trumpeters Bill Phillips and Stuart Laughton, Graeme Page on French horn, Gene on trombone, and Chuck on tuba. They were only rehearsing together, and weren't yet making a dime at it. But the seeds were sown. Gene has said, "When we started the quintet we had to believe that this was a serious venture, and not just for fun. After all, I had a family to support and a dog to feed. At first I was still making a living free-lancing, but sure looked for the day when the quintet would be my full-time livelihood."

Lady Luck has always smiled on the Canadian Brass. That's not to say that their career hasn't been defined by hard work, but there are times when a fortuitous break can make all the difference. For them it didn't happen in New York, or Hollywood, or even Toronto. The Brass began their leap to the big time, or rather the bigger time, in Hamilton, Ontario.

The Ontario Arts Council had recently become committed to supporting educational activity in the province. Gene and Chuck had been pursuing every available opportunity and scheduled a meeting with Robert Sunter, music officer of the Council, in which they tried to persuade him of the role they might play in furthering the organization's educational aims. At about this same time a woman named Betty Webster had begun an innovative program with the Hamilton Philharmonic, involving the resident players in that orchestra in an ambitious outreach program into the schools. She had a woodwind ensemble and a string quartet to work with. Betty called Bob Sunter, asking if he might be able to suggest a brass ensemble. "Well, as a matter of fact, there was a group in here just the other day..." It was soon a done deal, and the Canadian Brass found themselves the resident brass section of the Hamilton Philharmonic, with the opportunity to play a full schedule of appearances for Ontario's school children. As odd and unglamourous as it may seem, it was exactly what the Brass needed.

The move to Hamilton gave the group a practical plan for staying together and making a living at it at the same time. It was almost all too good to believe, except that the "revolving door plan" continued briefly. A trumpet opening arose when Stuart Laughton left to start a degree at the Curtis Institute of Music. Gene had remained in contact with his old friend, Fred Mills, and while Fred still couldn't join them, he did recommend another trumpet player— this was none other than Ron Romm. Ron was living in New York at the time, having just finished a master's degree at Juilliard, and was a busy free-lancer, but was itching to get out of the city. Ron came and played an audition with the Brass, and another major link in the quintet's future chain of events was clinched. Ron moved to Hamilton and began playing with the Canadian Brass in 1971.

Chuck had been commuting back and forth to Hamilton from his teaching job at the University of Toronto, but when that became impossible, he left the university and moved to Hamilton in 1972. The revolving door turned once more when Bill Phillips left the group. The Brass tried Fred one more time. By this time Fred believed that there really might be something to this quintet business, even though he had an enviable life playing in the orchestra in Ottawa, with a government pension and a tenured teaching position at the university. Finally persuaded, he moved to Hamilton to join the Canadian Brass. (The Brass claims they saved Fred from steady and certain boredom.) Click. With the right people in place, with modest opportunities before them, and with more creative energy than twenty normal civilians, the Canadian Brass was poised for success, and so what if that meant playing in the schools of Ontario for the time being?

The Brass took the school appearances very seriously—well, as seriously as they take anything. Other groups might have walked through them just for the money, or half-heartedly made an attempt to connect with the kids. The Canadian Brass quickly realized that children were the best possible audience for them at the time. Kids are honest, with a short attention span, but once they've been won over they are keen listeners and very supportive fans. In the five years between 1972 and 1977 the quintet played hundreds and hundreds of appearances in Canadian schools, for kindergartens through high schools, racking up over three hundred such performances in a single

The first true edition of the Canadian Brass,1970-1971:
(from left) Bill Phillips, Stuart Laughton, Chuck Daellenbach,
Graeme Page, Gene Watts

1971, Laughton
leaves, Ronald
Romm joins.

1972, Frederick Mills replaces Phillips.

Cover photo for first album, 1973

year. Chuck says, "To this day Gene can find the teacher's lounge in any school in the world. He just follows the smell of the bad coffee." All the while they were weaving in new repertory, and out of necessity were finding the light touch for which they've become famous. Gene speaks:

> We didn't set out to do choreography, or comedy between the numbers. It just evolved because it was what the audience needed. Maybe we just didn't want them to figure out how tired we were, and that we simply needed a break. Every day at lunch we would analyze what was good and bad about the morning appearance. The afternoon concert would then be the experiment, trying out the new ideas that came up at lunch. We did that for each performance for years. The challenge was to play a four-and-a-half minute piece by Bach and have them actually attentive and not throwing paper airplanes or shooting squirt guns or whatever. When we started performing for adult audiences, we found that what had worked best with the kids worked for the adults as well. It was great, too, because it saved us the trouble of putting together a whole new act.

The Canadian Brass may well be the first major international musical act in history to have gotten their start by appearing in public schools. It's a quaint spin on the familiar stories of countless musicians who have begun their careers by singing and playing in churches.

As if playing in an orchestra, doing community concerts, and running around Ontario nearly every day playing in schools wasn't enough, the Brass launched yet another innovative pursuit during their Hamilton years. Called the Hamilton Institute, the venture was headed up by Chuck and Gene, and strove to give young professional musicians a creative direction in pursuing a performing career. It lasted two years, and had about a dozen musicians enrolled at a time. The aims were not only to focus on group support for issues about actually playing music, but to encourage the musicians to be bold in creating their own performing opportunities, something in which the Canadian Brass was expert. They also stressed finding ways to fully connect with an audience in performance. In short, the institute was addressing all the crucial issues of making a life performing that are never taught in music schools.   It's safe to say that there has never been a radical educational program quite like it anywhere—after all, Chuck and Gene are hardly the stereotypical academic administrators. (The Canadian Brass still believes so strongly in their ideas that they continue to discuss plans for reviving the concept in a new incarnation at some point in the future.)

However charming and satisfying the school appearances were, it's not hard to understand that the Brass was getting restless to play for adults with money to spend on things like brass quintet concerts. They tried everything: shopping malls, happy hours at taverns, private parties, weddings, street corners...anyplace where there were people and live music was appropriate. They also started picking up a variety of studio work in Toronto, playing jingles, television scores, and radio work. The quintet began to get important concert work in Toronto, some of the first of which was performing with the Festival Singers of Canada, directed by Dr. Elmer Iseler. (In fact, the Brass' first tour of Europe was with this group in 1972. It's a relationship that has remained alive up to the present, with many collaborative performances and recording projects. Nearly every December the quintet collaborates with the Iseler Singers in concert, sometimes at Carnegie Hall.)

Almost from the first, because of Gene's contacts in Toronto, the quintet played radio broadcasts for CBC. The network had a mandate to create Canadian arts programming, and the Brass made very unusual and lively radio. Having been heard in cars and homes across Canada, it was only logical that the Canadian Brass would begin to book concerts. As everything else had been in their quick progression, it was just a natural outgrowth of their activities. With their increasing regional fame, the quintet was surprised to receive some memorable negative reactions not to their music, but to the group's name. At this time they were billed as the Canadian Brass Ensemble. They received a nasty letter from a player in the Toronto Symphony who claimed he had prior use of that name. (Since no one had ever heard of his group it couldn't have been that big a deal.) It was Betty Webster who suggested, "Why don't you just drop 'ensemble' and call yourselves 'the Canadian Brass'?" A couple of years later, a group in Montreal called themselves the Canadian Brass Quintet, and

First Kennedy Center Concert, 1975, with Larry and Marty Paikin, responsible for bringing the Brass to Hamilton

Jack McNie, Ontario cabinet minister, telling Chuck how the arts council really works, c. 1976.

even released an album under that name. But the old revolving door went around one more time, and this threat of confusion soon disappeared when the Montreal quintet folded.

Chuck tells the story of one further incident concerning the name game.

> We arrived at the performing hall in a small Nova Scotia college town to play a concert, and found that they had set up what looked like about 35 microphones and chairs all across the stage along with all this sound equipment. We looked at this, bewildered, and said, 'Thank you for all this, but frankly, 7 mikes and chairs per guy is a little more than we need.' There was complete confusion because the stage crew had no idea who we were. We soon learned that there was a local rock act that called themselves the Canadian Brass. And judging from the looks of things they must have been the largest rock band in history.

This band also folded, and the name never again became a problem.

A look at the Brass' performance schedule from these early years reveals hardly a day off for months at a time. One particularly memorable appearance about that time was at a private party given by Tony Adamson, chairman of the Ontario Arts Council. The host owned some property on Lake Ontario appointed with several impressive buildings, including a barn that had been converted into a concert hall. The site was indeed beautiful, but the Canadian Brass remember the appearance for another and more important reason: it was the first time anyone had ever paid them more than their asking price. "Tony was so delighted with our concert that he paid us an extra $100. We couldn't believe it! Our elation quickly turned to business sense when we realized that we had better start raising our fees!"

Chuck has often been quoted as saying, "It's important that people get involved in the music. We feel a responsibility to see to it that the audience has fun. A good performance isn't enough—people have to go out feeling happy." (He insists he can't remember ever saying this.) The Brass' aim toward "audience happiness" has led them to delve into all sorts of music for their concerts. At the time the quintet began, there was virtually no literature for brass quintets to play. There was only a small body of pieces, mostly by contemporary composers, and almost without exception they were not appropriate for what the Canadian Brass had in mind. Fueled by their response to audiences and creative thinking, they began to make transcriptions for brass quintet of all sorts of music, from Bach to ragtime. It seems a very simple step now, but was largely unprecedented. Every member of the quintet tried his hand at transcribing, and some of those early transcriptions are still in their current repertory. Fred Mills showed a talent for transcription, and in the early years became the Brass' principal arranger. "It was strictly out of necessity," Fred explains.

> We'd be out doing a performance somewhere and get the idea that a new piece would sound great for us, or that we needed a new piece of music to suit a special need in the program. I enjoyed doing that kind of thing, and just simply sat down and quickly did it most of the time. You have to remember that I had been immersed in quintet playing for a long time, and had those sounds and techniques very much in my head.

The Canadian Brass got another break relatively early in the life of the group in the form of a recording contract, something normally unheard of for a chamber ensemble. (Their recording history is only mentioned here; a later chapter has been devoted to that topic.) It was still further proof that the idea of a brass quintet maintaining a thriving, successful professional career wasn't as crazy as some might have thought. They were discovering in fact what they had always known in theory, that there were audiences who loved brass music.

Although according to the Canadian Brass they have always basically managed their own career, for business and publicity reasons they have sought out professional management at all points over the years, resulting in a succession of business relationships. When they began, there was really no appropriate management in existence in Canada. After they began their relationship with Elmer Iseler, they signed with the Maxwell Agency, which was also representing Iseler's choral group. The agency's principal client at the time was an international curling competition (!) sponsored by Air Canada. They had stumbled into managing a music group with the Iseler singers, and thought they'd take a chance with another in signing the Canadian Brass. Not surprisingly, the relationship didn't last long, since the

With Canadian choral master Elmer Iseler in the 1970s

1983,
with
Martin
Hackleman
on horn

agency knew everything about curling but nothing about music. Nevertheless, the Brass had formed a positive working relationship with one of their creative people, Christine Smith. As happens very often in this type of business, Chris formed her own agency and took the Brass as her first and only client. Her forte was in writing flashy publicity material, and with that in hand, along with reviews from across Canada, plus a couple of Canadian label albums in release, they headed to New York to seek out a little more fame and fortune.

They may have become a hot item in Canada, but looking for New York management that would take them seriously was quite a different matter. "A brass quintet—puh-lease, you gotta be kidding!" They spent their fair share of time sitting in waiting rooms, being brushed off from one person to another. No one seemed to think there was any point in taking a chance on something called a brass quintet. But as usual, a break wasn't far off. Kazuko Hillyer, head of one of classical music's premiere agencies, agreed to take the quintet onto her roster. She fell in love with the photo of the quintet on the album cover of their first (Canadian) release, and got musical approval of the group from her husband, Raphael Hillyer of the Juilliard Quartet. The Brass thought they had found the yellow brick road, but their hopes were temporarily dimmed when they got their first American booking from their big league New York agency: a 100-seat hall in Macon, Georgia. The fee was low, but Ms. Hillyer assured them that it was a start and better things would come of it. With a small chip on their shoulders the Canadian Brass headed to Georgia for their concert, fully realizing that they were probably losing money on the trip. They got a giant serving of humble pie when the tiny hall was only half full for the performance. While in Canada they had become a known quantity, in the U.S. they were not only unknown, they were downright obscure. Canadian what? What's a brass quintet anyway?

Their American career wouldn't languish for long. Their first appearance in New York occurred at a special 1976 "Antidote to the Bicentennial" concert presented by composer Peter Schickele (P.D.Q. Bach), who had written for them "the world's first opera for brass," *Hornsmoke*. This first New York appearance for the

Brass was hardly their ticket to fame and fortune. Amid the hijinks of the evening, when Schickele announced that a group called the Canadian Brass would perform an "opera" based on American myths of the West, well, more than a few in the audience might have thought that the whole thing was just a joke, including the idea of a group called the Canadian Brass. *Hornsmoke* did prove to be a hit, though, and remains in the Brass' repertory to this day. It's a spoof of hundreds of old movies about the mythical frontier of the West. (Chuck has stated that he believes it to be the great American opera, just edging out *Porgy and Bess.*) About that same time Ms. Hillyer, along with the Brass' Canadian manager at that time, David Haber, hosted a luncheon for delegates attending a convention of concert booking agents in New York, allowing the quintet to perform for all the major presenters in the U.S. at once. One member of the audience, hearing the Brass for the first time, became an important figure of for the next 15 years in their career. The man was Jim Murtha, whose New York public relations agency, Gurtman & Murtha Associates, has handled publicity for some of the biggest names in classical music—James Galway, Luciano Pavarotti, and Placido Domingo among them. With a major public relations firm on their side, the Brass' U.S. career was ready to take off.

Interestingly enough, though, the single most important event in really launching the quintet's performing career in the U.S. was an otherwise obscure 1977 appearance in San Antonio at the convention of an organization that books concerts into colleges and universities across the country. This was an innovative move, suggested by Maurine O'Neil of the Hillyer agency. Chuck relates:

> For hours and hours there were nonstop showcases of talent, almost all of which were rock bands and an occasional dance troupe. Before we went on they told us that we were to play for 20 minutes and not a second more, or they would pull the plug. They didn't even realize that we didn't have a plug to pull. It was really a musical meat market, with two performing areas on stage, one for the act that was on, and one for the act setting up to immediately go on next. It was well after midnight when we came out. I think we were the only acoustic group in the entire convention, and those people were glad to get a break from overamplified rock. We made quite an impression. As a result of that 20 minute audition, if you can call it that, we had 60 U.S. concerts booked for the next concert season. Very nice

"P.D.Q. Bach," a.k.a Peter Schickele, composer of *Hornsmoke*, the cowboy opera for brass.

tours. And in the middle of a twenty-eight day tour was our solo concert New York debut at the 92nd Street Y, which was wonderful for us. By the time we got there it was just another concert rather than a big deal. We were too busy playing a concert a day for 14 days before that New York date to get nervous about it.

This period, 1977 and 1978, was critical in the career of the Canadian Brass. In a bold move, their manager, Kazuko Hillyer, had signed a 15-year lease on a Broadway theatre, the Beacon, and the Brass actually made a Broadway debut playing a week's run of concerts there. (A side story to that Broadway run is that on one evening, for some reason, a representative from the musician's union was not admitted backstage. The Canadian Brass was actually brought up on charges by the union, in which they were found blameless except for one: apparently Fred walked past the union representative without saying hello, and was charged with "failing to greet a brother.")

In this same time period there was the invitation to tour the People's Republic of China, the first such tour by any western musical ensemble in that country for twenty years. That event alone blazed the Brass into international headlines around the world. Another milestone was signing with RCA, the first major record label for the quintet, after several albums in Canada. (Both these important career moves are are dealt with in detail in subsequent chapters.)

By the end of their first decade, the Canadian Brass was unstoppable. They had several record albums in release in wide distribution, had played a successful debut at Carnegie Hall (April 22, 1980), had toured Japan, and were playing over 100 sold-out concerts each year in major cities across the U.S. and Canada. They had been hailed by some of the world's most important critics, and had gained the reputation of being the hottest "crossover" act in the business.

Since the quintet's management history has been discussed in this chapter, it seems appropriate to insert an update on this subject. In the early 1980s the Canadian Brass had again changed managements, signing with Columbia Artists Management. In 1992 the group began a new relationship with IMG Artists for

1986, Hackleman out, David Ohanian in.

worldwide representation, joining a roster of prominent stars in the concert world.

One last mention of the old "revolving door." The roster of the Canadian Brass has been remarkably stable for the last twenty years, but there have been two changes in personnel since Fred joined the group in 1972. In 1983, after thirteen years of playing French horn with the quintet, Graeme Page left for other pursuits. He was replaced by Marty Hackleman, who came to the Brass from the Vancouver Symphony. Marty's tenure in The Canadian Brass lasted from 1983 until 1986. At that time David Ohanian, who had been a founding player in the Empire Brass Quintet, became the French horn member of the Canadian Brass, and Marty then took up David's spot in Empire Brass for two years before heading back to the Vancouver Symphony. (This swap was, understandably, big news in the brass world at the time.) When asked about the change of horn players, Gene shrugs his shoulders and smiles.

Well, you know, French horn players are really a different breed from the rest of us brass players. They have a totally different kind of instrument that requires a totally different technique from playing trumpet, trombone or tuba. And maybe—just maybe they have a different attitude, too, that might come from all the great solo literature that's been written for them and all the great orchestra parts they get to play. I mean, in orchestra literature they're often getting to be a hero playing some famous, noble solo, and we're sitting in the back row counting our 242nd measure of rest. We have come up with rules for hiring horn players over the years: they have to look dashing and far more photogenic than the rest of us, and they have to wear a size 40 suit. And it's worked well for us to have scrupulously high standards like this in the job description.

CHUCK DAELLENBACH

Did you come from a musical family?

Chuck: *(he speaks in an intelligent, boyish manner, with a trace of an accent from his northern Wisconsin roots)* Yeah, I did. A virtual small town musical dynasty of sorts. My dad was a band director, and I had two older sisters who were musicians. My oldest sister was a fantastic cellist and pianist—a prodigy really. She also played oboe in the band at school, and my younger sister played flute and piano. Dad was band director at school, and conducted two or three church choirs beyond that. Everyone in our family sang in choirs at church and school. My dad had a men's choir that was a pretty hot little group in our small town. Growing up in that household, it was fairly obvious that the odds were much better that I would become a musician than a star athlete. Although star athlete would have been fun too. I think nature had a say in that one. *(laughs)* Anyway, I started playing cornet in the first grade, but I think I was too young. I picked up the trombone in fourth grade, and also played lots of other instruments all through school, trying out everything really.

Where did you grow up?

Chuck: Rhinelander, Wisconsin. It's a small town in the northern part of the state.

How did you begin playing tuba?

Chuck: My grandfather played the violin in dance bands, but was also a tuba player. In my grandparents' house they had a very nice, traditional Norman Rockwell kind of living room. We'd go there on Sunday afternoons after church, and right there, sitting next to the couch there was always this very prominent tuba. So playing the tuba was sort of a family tradition. My

23

whole childhood was really a wonderful musical time for me. My dad was always going to workshops and clinics in the summers, and I would tag along on those trips, and would meet musicians from all over the Midwest. Dad would be playing all day in these clinics with all these band directors, and I would just play along with all the adults. So when it came to playing in band in school, I wound up being kind of a star student. When I was in seventh grade they needed me to play baritone in the eighth and ninth grade band, so I got out of arithmetic every day to do that. I'd get the assignment at the beginning of class, and as long as I did the homework and did O.K. on the tests, the teacher was very supportive. I remember that teacher saying to the class, "Chuck is unusually talented, and I'm sure we're going to be hearing a lot about him some day." I'm sure the other kids weren't too crazy about seeing me get out of math class. (laughs) Then when I was in ninth grade, the high school band needed a tuba player. They had four guys playing tuba, but they really weren't able to keep up with the music that the band was playing, so my dad arranged for me to play in his band a year early, and I was trudging up from junior high to play at the high school. It's pretty weird, this whole idea of being an accelerated band student. I mean, when we hear about accelerated students, it's always in math or science or something—some precocious genius who's doing nuclear physics at the age of 12 or something. It's not the kind of thing you usually think of for a tuba player. (laughs) But it was great for me. When I was a senior in high school my sister, Rosie, was in college at Ripon, Wisconsin, and they needed a tuba player. So for their spring concert I drove over there to play in the college band as a high school student. And it didn't stop there. When I went to college I wound up in an accelerated program where I actually started as a sophomore by going to Eastman two summers while I was still in high school. I was certainly an ambitious little tuba player, wasn't I?

How was is that you chose Eastman?

Chuck: My mother was actually responsible for that. My father had gone to Eastman for a summer course and had worked with a fellow named Everett Gates. Gates headed the music education department at Eastman. Dad was a diligent, interested

above: Evidence of
at least one day on
the junior high
football team, front
row, third from
right

right: Temporarily
trading in tuba for
baton as high
school Drum Major

participant in that course, and he and Gates had become friends. A few months later they were again together at the Midwest Band and Orchestra Clinic in Chicago, which was and still is a very major event in the instrumental world. My parents happened to sit next to Everett Gates in a clinic being given by a very well-known tuba player. A few minutes into the session my mother leaned over to Gates and whispered, "My son plays better than he does." Now, maybe this was true, but I think that there was a lot of mother love involved. But Mr. Gates thought enough of her comment to say, "Well, you'd better have your son get in touch with us at Eastman." On the basis of that whispered conversation at an otherwise forgotten tuba clinic, I sent in an audition tape and as a junior in high school was accepted into this accelerated music program. As I said, I went there two summers, and when I started college full-time, which should have normally been my freshman year, I had enough credits to be a sophomore.

And you stayed at Eastman for all of college and your graduate degrees?

Chuck: Sure. Hey, it was a lot easier than having to reapply at another school. *(laughs)*

Who did you study with at Eastman?

Chuck: My teacher there was a fellow named Don Knaub, a highly respected bass trombone player. He had tuba students in half a dozen major symphonies. Concurrent with that, I also studied with Arnold Jacobs in Chicago every summer. I had originally met Jake at a workshop in Colorado that my dad attended, and again, I tagged along. Boy, the way I tell it, it sounds like I spent all my youth going to band workshops with my dad! *(laughs)* But actually, all those clinics with my dad were quite a large factor in my development in those days. Anyway, we were in Colorado, and I had the chance to study with two of the most prominent tuba teachers in the world—Bill Bell and Arnold Jacobs. Encountering Arnold Jacobs was really a once in a lifetime kind of revelation for me, just as it has been for so many others. Like Paul on the Damascus road or something. I mean, dramatic! This man was a great natural teacher who could have

27

probably taught anything, but who just happened to be a wind specialist. He's the kind of legendary teacher that Liszt was for pianists of the nineteenth century. I think every serious wind player has made a pilgrimage to Chicago at some point to have a lesson or two with Arnold Jacobs. It's like a required rite of musical passage. I feel very lucky to have met him at such a young age, and I kept studying with him for years after that. In fact, I think that's one thing that brought Gene and me together, because he'd also been a student of Jake.

You finished a Ph. D. at Eastman by the time you were twenty-five, which is a pretty unusual accomplishment. Had you planned to go straight through from bachelor's to master's to doctorate from the outset?

Chuck: Since I had begun college in that accelerated way, I had finished my bachelor's degree by the time I was twenty. Continuing right into the master's program was a natural thing to do. I was too young to really consider doing much of anything else at that point. Besides, I liked Eastman, and wanted to continue there. I was fortunate to have two very supportive advisors, both of whom are very important names in music education. I've already mentioned Everett Gates, who was not only a brilliant music educator, but also had a phenomenal scientific mind. He worked with the C. G. Conn Corporation in the 40s and 50s in their legendary experimental laboratories. He was a key figure in the development of the Strobe-o-Conn, which was a revolutionary electronic tuning device—really the standard equipment that every band and orchestra used until the transistor age. And he was involved in projects like the first padless saxophone, plus a myriad of other musical inventions. This man has an incredible mind. To this day he can tell you the Köchel number for every piece Wolfgang Mozart ever wrote. Not only that, but he can tell you everything about a piece—the form and structure, and the exact date when he first heard it and who was playing and what they wore and what he'd had for breakfast that day and what the weather was like. Really an amazing mind! He pushed his students very hard, always encouraging us to find our full potential. And he stressed that musical accomplishment was much more of a matter of hard work than natural talent. He was

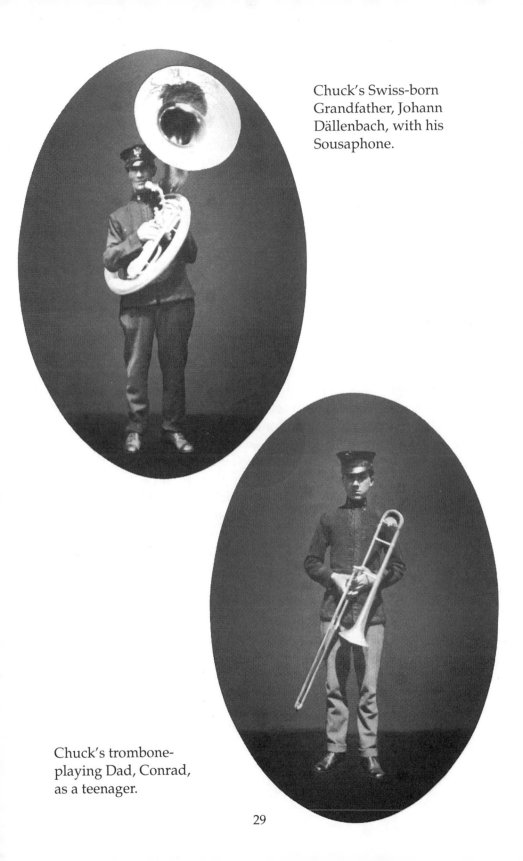

Chuck's Swiss-born Grandfather, Johann Dällenbach, with his Sousaphone.

Chuck's trombone-playing Dad, Conrad, as a teenager.

a very powerful influence on me. I also worked with Dr. Donald Shetler, who is very well-known in the education field for his pioneering work in educational technology. He was in on the ground floor in developing the whole concept of instructional television, microwave systems and all that. A very interesting fellow. He'd been a jazz pianist and a very fine cellist before specializing in education, and had all those traits one likes in a musician, which is lots of broad and developed interests in addition to being a very fine musician. So you can probably tell by the way that I talk about them that I really admired these two men, and I related very well to both Shetler and Gates.

Your focus at that time then was music education?

Chuck: Yeah, and at that time I was really into it. About that time the NDEA [National Defense Education Act], used to give grants for aspiring, gifted teachers. They decided to expand the program into music education, and chose music students from three schools nationwide to receive these education grants. I got one of those, and that's what took me all the way through the Ph. D. I'm really glad that it worked out that way, because I had auditioned and been accepted into the Army Band, but then the grant came along, and allowed me to go into the doctoral program rather than the Army. Which was perfectly fine with me, believe me! The doctorate I got actually should have been called an E. Ed., but Eastman didn't have such a degree. So I wound up with a Ph. D., which sounds like I should know something about philosophy. All I can muster up in that regard is that I'm philosophic about the fact that I don't know anything about philosophy. *(laughs)*

What was your dissertation topic, by the way?

Chuck: My master's thesis had been "Observable teaching behaviors as identified by the use of portable videotape recorders." Wait, was that it? Well, whatever, it was something very academic and impressive sounding. Looking back, maybe it should have been "Planning encores for brass quintet concerts in Tokyo" or "Observable behaviors in booking brass concerts on four continents," but I don't think my advisors would have approved those topics. *(laughs)* For the doctoral dissertation I just continued research in the same vein, but with a different twist. The focus was on "Observable learning behaviors using portable videotape recorders." It became an instant international bestseller, by the way. Actually, as obscure as those research topics might sound, they were really fascinating to me. And all that training in music education has proven to be very applicable to lots of my work with the Canadian Brass—all our school appearances, the Hamilton Institute that we started in the 70s, our clinics with brass students, our publications for brass players, and our new commitment to the whole idea of adopting a school and giving something back to music education. I've often made light of the Ph. D., and spoken of it as a useless bit of over achievement. But I've never really believed that. In all honesty, I have to say that I've become more and more proud of my education.

You certainly must have been a diligent student to have gone so far so quickly.

Chuck: My dad had given me the best tips for avoiding the "Black-Eye Special," which was his term from the '30s for the train that took you home after being thrown out of college: Always sit at the very front, don't miss any classes, and always look interested even when you aren't. It must have worked. Eastman gave me a tough discipline at a crucial time in my life. I was an expert at going to school. And I don't just mean accomplishing the work for the required courses. I mean, I studied those curriculum requirements so thoroughly that I would have gotten an A+ in getting through a doctoral program in a swift and orderly fashion. I discovered that there were courses that you could take in the master's degree that wouldn't apply to the doctorate. Of course, they didn't tell you that until later. But I figured it out and certainly steered clear of those credits. I only made one mistake along the way. I enrolled in a course in film scoring—don't ask me why, because I have a better talent to become an astronaut than to score a movie—and was in the class for a month when I realized that the credits wouldn't carry forward into the doctoral degree. I transferred into a counterpoint class so quickly that I think I must have left tread marks! *(laughs)* When it came time for my final orals, the two

Hear no evil

Smell no evil

Geez—virtue can be so dull.

teachers I mentioned earlier, Gates and Shetler, were there on my committee. And it was a good thing, too. I supposedly wound up with a minor in music history and music theory, heaven forbid, and so there were representatives on the orals committee grilling me on those subjects. I was defending my dissertation, and Gates and Shetler were there defending me. I remember one particularly tough question during the orals, and Don Shetler just audibly saying to one of his colleagues, "I'm sure glad nobody asked me that." *(laughs)* They were just persuasive enough to get me through.

Had you continued performing while you were in school?

Chuck: Oh sure. I was constantly still playing, in bands or in brass quintets. When my buddies in college were playing in dance bands, I couldn't exactly go that route with a tuba. So I was always putting together brass quintets in those days, and actually made some money at it. We'd book into these performances in schools and such, and actually beat out the group from the Rochester Philharmonic for those jobs. Even back then I guess I was the hustling businessman.

When you left Eastman did you aspire to an orchestra job?

Chuck: Sure. I wouldn't have minded getting an orchestra job. I just didn't get one. I auditioned for a couple, but without a lot of enthusiasm. I'd just never been very motivated to learn the excerpts in the right way for those auditions. I like to be in a situation where I can play a lot, and those orchestra parts for tuba are pretty sparse. There's just not enough there. A string player will get a part book for a symphony that's twenty-five pages, and the tuba part is what? Two or three pages? It's both very demanding and very boring. It has been said that tuba parts in orchestral works are either so difficult that nobody can play them, or so easy that anyone can play them. There's seldom a middle ground. And you rarely get a chance to be a hero. It's certainly not the rush that playing principal horn is, for example. Even back in high school, in the concert band we'd play all of this very advanced, meaty music—transcriptions of orchestra pieces like the "Rienzi Overture," or difficult original material for concert band—and then I'd go to the orchestra rehearsals and we'd play "Jingle Bells" or watered down arrangements of show tunes because that's all that the string players could handle at our school. It drove me crazy! I don't mean to sound totally down on playing in orchestras. While I was at Eastman I did very much enjoy playing under Howard Hansen and Walter Hendl in the orchestra there. But I love playing constantly, and that's why I was always so much happier in concert bands or in brass chamber groups. You have a fundamental bass line that's almost always there and is an indispensable feature of the music.

Where did you go from Eastman?

Chuck: I joined the music faculty at the University of Toronto. I conducted a couple of bands, taught courses in music education, and taught whatever tuba players were around. It was fun, because I was very close in age to my students. In Canada they have a grade 13 in high school, and college is a five year program, so by the time they graduate they're about 24 years old, and I was only 25 at the time I began teaching. As you might imagine, I wasn't an entirely conventional music professor. I was teaching a tuba class to fourth year music education majors, and decided that since these people would be teaching themselves very soon, I would allow them to evaluate themselves and determine their own grade. I had little conference appointments with each student, and they played for me and we chatted about what we had covered in class. I figured that if they gave themselves a low mark, that they probably deserved it. At first the students were very modest and fair. But the word must have gotten out about what was going on, because by the end of the day they all were saying firmly that they thought they deserved an A for the course. I think I'm still known in Toronto for that free-thinking semi-disaster! *(laughs)* But it was fun. I was at the university as a full-time faculty member for two years, until I joined Gene and the Brass full time, but continued to teach tuba students there for several years after that. I had to stop when our performing schedule just got too crazy. I couldn't exactly phone in my lessons from China or Texas or wherever. Students really do need regular attention, and as much as I loved it, I had to let it go.

When did you meet Gene?

Chuck: Almost before I started teaching at the university in 1970. I had auditioned and gotten a job playing free-lance in the Hamilton Philharmonic whenever they needed a tuba, which was an easy drive from Toronto. Gene had a brass group—the Canadian Brass Ensemble, in fact—that he was trying to get off the ground and was in residence in the orchestra at Hamilton. Actually, they were only a brass quartet at the time, because they didn't have a tuba player. He persuaded the management·at Hamilton that they needed a full-time, resident tuba player in what was really a chamber orchestra. It was a bit far-fetched perhaps, but it worked out, and allowed me to join the Brass and leave my teaching job. It was an exciting change of direction for me, and really allowed me to begin to show my true colors. The idea of performing in what was a top-flight, professional brass quintet for a living was right up my alley. Who could have ever guessed that a tuba player could have the kind of performing career that I've had since then? It boggles the mind.

You handle most of the group's business affairs, don't you?

Chuck: Well, someone's got to do it. *(laughs)* I have to admit, I get a charge from all of that activity—negotiating contracts with management, working out record deals, figuring things out with our publicist, running our publishing activities, hashing through things with the lawyers, and putting together whatever deals need to be made. I'm always looking for what opportunities are on the horizon for us, and then trying to realize them in the most advantageous way possible. It's really a tremendous benefit to be in charge of your own destiny, like we've always been, rather than just playing in some ensemble where someone else is controlling the shots. Maybe I like the rush of wheeling and dealing a little bit. When things are moving forward at a quick pace it can be very exciting. Like in 1989 when we left CBS and negotiated the record deal with Philips. That came up very quickly, almost out of nowhere, and was really a thrilling deal to watch come together. Then again, there are those times when things get bogged down in complexities, and it can be very frustrating. But I can handle the inevitable frustrations. I'm used to it by now.

And it's not like I make these decisions in a vacuum. I'm constantly in consultation with the other guys on all these matters, and Gene particularly plays a very active role as a partner with me in all of our negotiations.

That group dynamic must be a prominent factor in the success of the Canadian Brass, and a real strength in making decisions.

Chuck: I think the idea of a cooperative group of individuals is a wonderful thing, and we've usually made it work in a very satisfying way. A group gives you an excellent sounding board in the whole collaborative process. If you have an idea, and you can't get one other person on your side, you save the embarrassment of going outside the group with that idea. We're shielded from that kind of embarrassment. An idea comes up, gets batted around, and if everyone else thinks it's a terrible idea, then it just harmlessly disappears. Now if the guy feels strong enough about it he'll bring it up again, but until he can get at least one other person to see the merits of his scheme, then it won't be something we're going to act upon. It absolutely permeates everything with us—a choice of a piece of music, the choice of an arranger, management, record companies, whether we need a vacation, whether a certain gig should be taken, or whether we add other players in a concert and who those players will be, what color tie we should wear in performance, and on and on. This kind of group deliberation has really been a safety net for us all these years. In a way, that process has kept us around so long. I think our staying power is that we are constantly evaluating and re-evaluating not only what we're doing, but what we've done and how we can improve it. We've done this since day one. And I can tell you, it can get tough on the the psyche to constantly, constantly be going over things like this. It's much easier to let things rest. But it's really what has kept us moving forward all these years.

With the kind of schedule you guys keep, do all the concerts run together after a while, or do you remember particular ones?

Chuck: Well, I couldn't pretend to remember all of them individually, but lots of them do hang around in my mind as

above: With tuba fan Cyndi Lauper.
below: Is that Billy Graham?

absolutely specific events. What's the university in Salt Lake City? Must be Brigham Young, right? Well, we had this show there a few years ago, and Chuck might have been just a little sick. In fact, Chuck was more than a little sick. I remember we flew in—in my case it was more like "flu" in—and all this scenery was racing by as they drove us to the university from the airport, and it could have been Peru as far as I was concerned. There were a few unscheduled stops as I recall. The other guys went to the hall to set up, and the driver took me to a doctor. I remember him telling me that whatever he gave me would fix me right up—tomorrow. Someone got me to the hall, and I was in some kind of semi-comatose state. It came time for the show, and the guys woke me up and wound me up and pulled me out on stage. For the time I was performing I was relatively normal, mustering all my strength and adrenaline, being momentarily healed by the audience's energy and the whole situation. Miracle cure, right? Wrong. The moment I stepped off stage at the intermission I collapsed into a heap again. I went out like a light, and somehow got through the second half. After the show I quickly changed into my street clothes, turned out the lights, and fell on a couch in the dressing room while everyone else went off to a reception. Well, Gene, tells the tale of an eager young tuba player who showed up backstage and found his way to my dressing room. He comes in and pulls up a chair beside my deathbed, and bursts into a barrage of quick-fire questions, like only a kid can do: "So what kind of mouthpiece do you use? Is that a Schilke mouthpiece? What size is it? And that horn of yours is absolutely incredibly cool, man!" He's all wound up, going through his enthusiastic spiel, and I'm lying there with my eyes half closed, wondering whether I was going to barf all over the poor kid. I guess that's the price of fame and fortune as a tuba player, huh? All I could think about was: I'm going to die alone with a fourteen-year-old tuba player in a dark dressing room in Salt Lake City and my last words will be, "Yeah...it's...it's a... a Schilke."

F R E D   M I L L S

How did your musical life begin?

Fred: *(he typically talks quickly, in sharp, energetic bursts)* My brother took piano lessons when I was very young. I think I must have been about 3 or 4 years old. He's 11 years older than me. I can remember all the tunes he played, things like "Für Elise" and "Danny Boy" and "Isle of Capri." He doesn't know this, but he probably was my first musical influence and he doesn't play piano anymore.

Did you wind up taking piano lessons too?

Fred: Yeah, I started with the same teacher he had. I loved the *idea* of playing the piano, but I just really detested taking lessons. It was a very uncomfortable experience. The teacher's name was Miss Pond, and she lived with her spinster school teacher sister. Their house always smelled of antiseptic and cocker spaniel. I remember that you had to take your shoes off when you entered the house and go up the back stairs to sit and wait for your lesson. I was so frustrated because she could not explain the difference between the bass and treble clefs to me. I was only 7 at the time, but I knew enough to know that this was pretty important stuff, and I just wasn't getting it. The lessons were very tedious, and I used to play hooky for months at a time. Then my mother bribed me to go to piano lessons by saying that she'd buy me a bicycle. So I got a bike, but then it seems the spring came and I wound up going off and riding my bike when I should have been in piano lessons. Mother gave up at that point and said, "Forget it, no more piano lessons!" Later, when I was 11, my buddy took up the cornet in the YMCA band. And believe it or not, it was the smells of a brass instrument that first made an impression on me. I remember him opening up the case—an old, musty, used cornet case—and the unique smells of an old horn, the oils, the spittle,

and that old case were a vivid introduction to the whole idea of being a brass player.

So you started on the cornet?

Fred: Uh-huh. The next thing you know, I was playing cornet in the same band as my friend. And it was the old situation where this guy went from town to town selling used instruments and organizing a band. As soon as he sold everything then he'd split, and there was no more band. It was straight out of *The Music Man,* except we didn't march down the street playing "Seventy-Six Trombones." *(laughs)* Anyway, that got me into it. Then I joined what they called a police boys' band in Guelph, which is where I grew up, a town about an hour from Toronto. This police boys' band was, for all intents and purposes, a way to take delinquent kids off the streets and keep them out of trouble. They gave you an instrument and a uniform and a band practice once a week. I loved it. It was so much more fun to play with the other guys than sitting alone practicing piano. Within the year, when I was 12, I was taking private lessons from the band director, this fine old British gentleman, Ted Denver, who had his roots in the Salvation Army and military bands. He taught me for free, and really treated me like the son he never had. I never actually participated in school band music because it just wasn't very developed where I grew up. So it was the police band and military bands and cornet solos—music like the "Zampa Overture," William Tell," "Light Cavalry," Sousa marches and British marches. The music was mostly British rather than American because in Canada the British tradition of brass bands predominated at that time. Later, when I was 15 or 16, I took up piano again because I had become seriously interested in music. I was studying theory in high school in a British-based Canadian syllabus of study. It wasn't very strict, but we did have a unified course of study with examinations at the end of the year. About that time I also became interested in jazz and switched to trumpet. I played in an all kids' dance band, what they called a Mickey Mouse band—a hotel band that played music like Guy Lombardo and Sammy Kaye. We had our own arrangements and our own uniforms, and we used to grab all the work from the older guys who had dance bands. We had a complete repertory

41

above: A department store appearance with his college band, Oneonta, New York, 1954. "We always had spending money and a car and records and clothes. None of my schoolmates had those things, except for a couple of other guys in the band. We were very popular!"

below: Guelph, Ontario, second from right

with one of everything: a polka, a cha-cha, a bright swing tune, a waltz set, and like that. It was quite a band!

Where did you go after high school?

Fred: Well, in my last years in high school I went to the New York State Music Camp in the Adirondacks, which exposed me to the school music system in the U.S. That was a fantastic experience for me! I got to play in concert bands, orchestras, and jazz bands with these kids from all over and discovered lots about music that I hadn't known before that time. I met Willard Musser there, who taught at Hartwick College, and he offered me a scholarship to come and study music. Musser was the first teacher to encourage me to pursue a professional career. So I went to Hartwick College in upstate New York and got a B.S. in music education.

What was college like?

Fred: I was really into jazz and had a band all through college. We worked clubs and lounges every weekend, so I always had spending money and a car and records and clothes. None of my schoolmates had those things, except for a couple of other guys in the band. We were very popular! *(laughs)* One of the most important events for me at that age was the first time I ever heard a professional symphony orchestra. I went down to a concert in Carnegie Hall on a Sunday afternoon and heard Mitropoulos conduct the New York Philharmonic. I remember the concert as if it were yesterday—I still have the program as a matter of fact. They played the Dvořák Symphony in G major. That afternoon really changed my life. I heard this phenomenal trumpet player in that orchestra, and I decided I had to study with him. So soon after that I went off to Juilliard and auditioned to study with William Vacchiano, who was first trumpet in the New York Philharmonic at the time.

Did your college teachers encourage you to go on to Juilliard, or was this something that you did on your own?

Fred: It was my idea. I first had tried to get into Curtis because I knew it was free tuition, but there wasn't enough money there for me, I guess, and they didn't accept me. Anyway, I wound up at Juilliard for three years, and as usual, when you go to Juilliard you're only one of many talented students. The school seemed quite big to me. It was uptown at that time near Columbia, the current site of the Manhattan School of Music. When I entered, there were twenty-four trumpet players competing for spots, and within the first year I jumped from twenty-third to eighth. In my second year I jumped to sixth. And in my third year it didn't really matter so much to me where I ranked in the school because I was doing a lot of jobbing at New York City Opera, New York City Ballet, and lots of other places. I was a very busy free-lancer, which was quite an achievement, because at Juilliard not many did that. The school frowned on students playing jobs and thought that you should concentrate on getting your degree. But I felt differently about it. I felt that this was a chance for practical experience, which was why I was in Juilliard in the first place. After all, it is a professional school. I also used to play in brass quintets at that time, simply because I enjoyed it so much. That whole time in the 1950s was really the beginning of brass chamber music. The New York Brass Quintet was already a role model, comprised of Harvey Phillips, Robert Nagel, John Swallow, Ted Weiss, and at that time, Johnny Barrows. I played two concerts and a recording with them, substituting for Ted. I was also playing in a professional brass quintet of guys from the New York City Opera Orchestra, and we were doing lots of Young Audience concerts. There was an association called "Young Audiences" that promoted instrumental music education in the schools, and it was funded by a trust fund and a private endowment. The head office was in New York, and that brass quintet I played in was a flagship group in that organization. I was quite a bit younger than all the other guys and was the only student in the group. We used to do two or three school shows a week, and I remember that we also did a TV show. This was what I was doing all during my last year at Juilliard. I barely made classes, but I made all my lessons with Vacchiano, which were very inspiring. I spent a lot of time in the practice room, and a lot of time in the library listening to records and looking at scores. This all seemed much more interesting than my course work. I remember that I took a philosophy course that was especially disastrous! *(laughs)* By that time I'd had enough of taking classes, having spent 5 straight

The Contemporary Brass Quintet, New York, 1964
rear: Chuck Brady, Fred
front: Vince Schneider, Ron Manson, Dennis Smith

years in college. I never got into the orchestra at the school, but in my last summer there the Juilliard orchestra was invited to play at the 1958 World's Fair in Brussels. They asked me to play first trumpet on that tour because someone else had backed out. Besides Brussels we played in England, Germany, Italy, and one concert in Salzburg. That was an incredible experience for me! It was my first trip to Europe, and every time we tour there now I always think of that Juilliard trip because that was the beginning. I love going to Europe for that reason.

At the end of the summer did you go back to school?

Fred: Three months after I came back from Europe to New York I dropped out of Juilliard because of Stokowski. *(pause)* I guess I'd better explain that. At that time in New York there were several hundred musicians making a living free-lancing, playing everything but the New York Phil and the Met. On one of those jobs I was asked to play a concert for what I believe was the League of Composers, a concert conducted by Leopold Stokowski. It was a terrific orchestra playing all American music—Paul Creston, Hovhaness, Bernstein and Henry Cowell. At the break during rehearsal Stokowski walked back to the trumpet section—he rarely left the podium—to say hello to my mentor, Ted Weiss, who was a great help and got lots of work for me back then. The maestro said, "Mr. Weiss, I'm looking for a trumpet player to take to Houston." Stokowski was music director of the Houston Symphony at the time. Ted introduced me, saying "Maybe Fred would be interested in playing in Houston." Stokowski said, "Very good, would you come and play for me tomorrow afternoon at one o'clock?" So the next day I went to his Fifth Avenue apartment to play what I didn't really realize was a private audition. There were two other guys after the job, and he offered it to me that same afternoon. When Stokowski offers you a job, you don't exactly turn him down! It was early September, and I was just about to go back to school. I decided that playing trumpet in the Houston Symphony sounded a lot more fun than going to classes, or not going to classes in my case. So I signed a contract that week and resigned from Juilliard, if you can resign from Juilliard. At least I told them I wasn't coming back, and they were kind of upset because they'd given me a full scholarship after a lot of urging on my part. Here it was September, and the Houston season opened on October 12! It all happened so fast, but those things always do.

What was Stokowski like to play for?

Fred: He was a very inspiring musician. He was forever transcribing baroque music for a modern orchestra, and particularly had a reputation for rescoring Bach. My first year in Houston I performed quite a lot of those transcriptions, because he always programmed them. We did his rendition of *Pictures at an Exhibition*, or a rescored Bach cantata, or his version of the "Toccata and Fugue in D minor." I don't think he ever heard Canadian Brass play it, but if he had he'd have been really knocked out I think, because it's exactly in the spirit of the work he did. He was a very forward looking person, and thought that great music belonged to everyone, not just an elite few.

He did the music for Fantasia, *didn't he?*

Fred: Oh yes! He believed in reaching a lot of people. For three or four decades if someone mentioned "The Maestro" on the podium, they probably meant Stokowski. Walt Disney certainly projected that to the North American public.

How long did you play in the Houston Symphony?

Fred: I spent two orchestra seasons there, and then Stokowski quit the symphony and I came back to New York. Even while I was in Houston I would scurry back to New York in the off season and continue my free-lance activity. I never even let my apartment go in the city. When I came back to stay I did a lot of theatre work, ballet and opera, and became a permanent member of the New York City Opera Orchestra. In those days this was a very adventurous company in programming new pieces. Every spring they had a four week American opera season. I counted up once, and over six seasons I did something liked forty-three twentieth century operas, including various American pieces, Poulenc, Honegger, Stravinsky, and Menotti. It was was very interesting and inspiring. Then the company moved to Lincoln

Center and sort of started competing more with the Met, and there were far fewer contemporary operas in the repertory. The job became more of a job then, and I got more or less bored with it. But the opera season only lasted ten weeks in the fall and ten in the spring, so I had plenty of time to do other jobs. I played a lot for Robert Shaw, and did tours and recordings with him. I also did recording with Morton Gould and Stokowski. I must have made about ten records with Stokie as a free-lancer, and ten records was a lot in those days, because there wasn't that much orchestral recording going on in New York. I played under Bruno Walter as an extra with the New York Philharmonic, and in the off-stage band at the Met—you know, things like that. I continued playing with that brass quintet that I mentioned earlier, and got involved with another brass quintet that played nothing but contemporary music. It was all very eclectic and varied. I also played for Pablo Casals, and went to the Casals Festival about four springs in a row in the mid '60s to play in his "all-star" orchestra. I was involved in the Marlboro Festival in the summers, played in the Brooklyn Philharmonic, and was in the Met Chamber Orchestra series at the Met Museum. I did some jingles and film scores as well. A lot of the time I really had fun with all these endeavors, whereas many free-lancers treated everything like it was just a job. It's actually a luxury to be able to make a living playing music. I remember I had a very pleasant job playing at Jones Beach—do you know Jones Beach? It's just outside the city, on the south shore of Long Island. They used to produce musicals in an amphitheater there in the summer, and every night for ten weeks I played a light show called *Song of Norway*, which was music of Edvard Grieg adapted to a musical comedy. It was a huge cast and a wonderful production. I'd sit there and gaze up at the stars in the summer sky and think, "They're paying me to do this?" It was easy and lovely work, and a great pleasure. But eventually I got—I don't know if it was burned out—I think I just became disappointed with the lifestyle in New York. I did nothing for years but work seven days a week, because I never turned anything down. Some of it was interesting, and some of it wasn't, but you always took the uninteresting things to meet the financial potential. Eventually it got to be more of a financial reward than a musical reward. So when the opportunity arose for me to go back home to Canada I

above:
With Gerard
Schwarz,
conductor of the
Seattle
Symphony

right:
With John
Williams,
conductor of the
Boston Pops

jumped at the chance.

When was that?

Fred: I moved to Toronto in January of 1968 to become personnel manager and first trumpet at the National Ballet of Canada Orchestra. I met Gene that year, and we played together at the opera, the ballet, and at the Stratford Shakespeare Festival, which had quite a lively musical scene in the summer. Gene and I used to play brass quintets for kicks. We thought, "Well, you don't make money at this, but you play for yourself." So we'd pick up whatever players were around and would sit up late at night and go into the cellar of the Avon Theatre and play Pezel and Dahl and Gabrieli—any quintet music we happened to have. It's amazing that the thread goes back to that, because the Canadian Brass was not even in existence yet. The next year, 1969, I went off to Ottawa and took a job in the newly formed National Arts Center Orchestra offered to me by Mario Bernardi. It was the first of its kind in North America, a completely government subsidized chamber orchestra, and it was really a terrific group. It was put together from scratch to fill a void that existed in Ottawa when they built a new performing arts center and didn't have a resident symphony. So the orchestra filled that mandate, and also played in the pit for the opera, the ballet, and any visiting companies that came to Ottawa. It really became a national showcase. While I was there Gene and Chuck formed the Canadian Brass in Toronto, and they asked me to join them. I was bound by contract to stay in Ottawa, but I did tell them about another trumpet player I knew whom I thought was probably ripe to get out of New York. That was Ronnie Romm. I'd run into Ronnie a few times. He studied at Juilliard when I was playing at New York City Opera, and he used to play jobs with me here and there. In fact, I first met him out in Los Angeles years before when I was on vacation and he was playing at the Bowl. He was only 18 at the time, and playing with the L.A. Philharmonic. He'd just gotten a new Porsche and took me for a ride around the Hollywood Hills, and we wound up playing trumpet duets. When I found out what a great player he was I felt sure we'd run into one another again. Anyway, as I said, I recommended Ron to Gene and Chuck.

How did you wind up in the Canadian Brass?

Fred: Well, it seems that Gene and I were on the phone all the time, and he kept saying "come on, you gotta join us," and I kept saying "well, I don't know..." I had a terrific job in Ottawa. I taught at the university and played three days a week in this first class orchestra. The city is very beautiful. But the time was right for a change, so I gave notice at the orchestra and moved back to Toronto to join the Brass. In fact, three days after I joined them we were off to Europe on a tour, which kind of reminded me of when I latched onto that Juilliard tour back in 1958.

Did you have any doubts about making a full time living in a brass quintet?

Fred: I had nothing *but* doubts about it! But I was ready for it. After all those years of free-lancing in New York I had gotten kind of brave and accustomed to taking chances. It was an exciting time. We were the only brass quintet in Canada, where they weren't afraid of the concept of subsidizing the arts. They had formed the Canada Council, which subsidized all the orchestras across the country, plus the CBC designated so many hours for live music on the radio each week. And the Brass filled a bill in this scheme of things that was unique. We seized the opportunities that were available and created a few more on our own. And things have built ever since those early days. I don't think anything happened suddenly with us. It was always better every year. If we ever got discouraged, either individually or as a group—which hasn't happened very often—something would come along that was exciting. Like the 1977 China trip, or our first tour of Japan in 1980, or the Edinburgh Festival in 1981. It's always interesting to see what might come along next for us, because the past has proven that the future will always be full of surprises.

You've done more quintet arrangements than anyone else in the group.

Fred: Well, in the beginning it was out of necessity. At the time we were starting out most of the music arranged for brass quintet was pretty mediocre. We needed material, so I jumped in and wrote out some charts. I'm not really a creative arranger. What I do is transcribe existing classical pieces for quintet, or ragtime pieces. Most of the original music for brass quintet that existed when we started was not only too hard to play out on tour every night, it was also too dull to program. At that time nobody had ever taken the big classical hits like "Water Music" or the "Toccata and Fugue in D minor" and done them for brass quintet. We decided that this was what we needed on our concerts, so I did them. The price was right, because arrangers are expensive! *(laughs)* I also didn't feel that the trumpet parts had been done particularly well in other transcriptions I'd played, and so I wanted to do some things that worked well specifically for Ron and me. Some of the charts I did in those early years are still staples of our repertory. In fact, lots of other people are playing them because they're published now for anyone to buy and play. Some of the other work I've done for us is strictly because we needed something right away. Like in 1989 we played the national anthems at the Major League All-Star game with Doc Severinsen, so I scratched out some parts for that. But in the last ten years, since our touring schedule is so hectic, I haven't done as much transcribing. Recently I got a Macintosh Powerbook, and am back to transcribing on airplanes and in waiting rooms.

What would you be doing now if we weren't doing this interview? (As we talk to Fred it is a Saturday afternoon before an evening concert. The Brass is in San Diego doing a weekend series with the San Diego Symphony.)

Fred: I'd probably be down at the auto show with David. Or writing an arrangement on my portable computer. Or just strolling around the town getting some sun. Or checking out the pawn shops for old trumpets and cornets, which my wife, Louise, and I collect. I wouldn't go sailing, because that would take too much out of me. You don't want to distract yourself from your purpose for being here, yet you also don't want to just sit in the hotel and watch TV either. So it's everybody knowing his own thing. Gene and Chuck might be out doing antiques now, but come four or five o'clock they'll be back at the hotel. Between five and six we all pretty much do our thing, which is meditation, and

 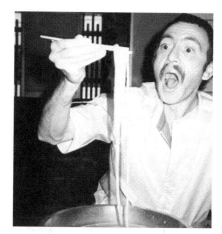

above: Working on his embouchure

below: Playing duets with wife Louise at their wedding in October of 1991.

rest so that we will have our wits about us for the concert in the evening. You have to conserve your energy and compact it into the performance in the evening. After all, the whole reason we're in St. Louis or Dallas or Minneapolis is to do that show, and if there's a little bit of free time, then it's a luxury. But you can't overextend yourself and abuse it.

Tonight you're playing with an orchestra. Is that different from your regular concerts?

Fred: The guest spots on orchestra concerts are only about ten per cent of our yearly activity. It's a nice change for us because it usually involves being in a place at least two days, rather than doing one-nighters. It's also nice to come in contact with lots of other musicians. We get to know a lot of the brass players in most of the North American orchestras. When we have return engagements with orchestras it's like meeting old friends again. Even when we've never played with an orchestra before there are usually a couple of familiar faces in the brass section. At rehearsal today I looked back and saw two young guys that we worked with when they were students, one we met six years ago in Indiana, and one last year at Eastman. It's fun to see their progress and to gather around and shoot the breeze. We catch up on what instrument they're playing and how their teacher's doing, and it becomes a very small community. You eventually get to know all the guys. And having lived in New York all those years, I met a lot of them then anyway, or at least their teachers. In those days I'd walk out of the stage door at City Opera and go up the street to the Carnegie Tavern. In the 1960s all the great orchestras played Carnegie Hall, and all the orchestra musicians gathered for a beer after the concerts. I knew everybody. I knew all the guys in the New York Phil, the London Symphony, the Chicago Symphony, the Philadelphia Orchestra, and lots of others. You'd worship some of these guys as great players, but you'd also get to know them as people. So that continues, only maybe we're a little older now, and some of the younger players think of us as role models of some kind. Maybe we've shown them what's possible for brass players. It's interesting that when we first started doing orchestra shows the guys in the back row would look at us like "Aw, what are they doing, mumble, mumble." But now in this concert tonight, for instance, we're bringing those guys up front, and they're getting far more audience recognition than normal.

When you were young, what trumpet players did you look to as role models?

Fred: Harry James. Louise actually played in his band the last year of his life, in the early '80s. Then when I got more into jazz it was Miles Davis and Dizzy Gillespie. Maynard Ferguson. In the symphony field it was my teacher, William Vacchiano, who played in the New York Philharmonic. He was also Ron's teacher, by the way. Bud Herseth in the Chicago Symphony. Gil Johnson in Philadelphia. Armando Ghitalla and Roger Voisin of the Boston Symphony.

I know you guys spend some time working with students and judging competitions.

Fred: We feel obligated to try to give back something to the younger players just coming up. There are so many good players around. And it seems to be happening all over, not only in the U.S. and Canada, but in Japan and Europe, too. For instance, the brass players in Scandinavia are fantastic! There are more amateur brass enthusiasts in Scandinavia than in any other part of the world.

I wonder why that's so.

Fred: Hmm ... it must be those long winters.

DAVID OHANIAN

Do you recall your first memories of music?

David: *(he speaks very deliberately and distinctly)* It probably goes back to before my conscious memory because both my parents were musicians. My father was the music director in the public school system I attended. My mother was a pianist and organist who played in church, accompanied for my dad's choir at high school, and taught piano lessons at home. So I guess it was natural that I started out on piano.

And this was where?

David: Westport, Connecticut. So I started on piano when I was 8 years old, and although I wasn't by any definition an outstanding pianist, I liked it well enough. By the time I was 10 I was playing trumpet, and in the two or three years after that I played most of the brass and woodwind instruments. I remember one day when I stayed home from school—I had a cold or something—and there was a saxophone in the living room that had just been repaired that Dad was going to take back to school. I found that new musical toy, and by the end of the day when he came home I could play the saxophone. I mean, I wasn't Charlie Parker or anything, but I had figured out where the notes were and could play some melodies. I just had an appetite and an affinity for learning different instruments at that age, although trombone always seemed silly to me.

Hear that, Gene?

David: Very awkward. *(laughs)* But French horn was really a challenge. I could get going pretty quickly on the other wind

The Ohanian
Family Trio,
Mom, Dad
and 12 year
old David
playing the
Brahms Horn
Trio.

Telecast of
concerto with
the Hartford
Symphony at
age 16

Tanglewood,
1961, third
horn from
left.

instruments, but playing horn was like walking on egg shells. I started horn when I was 11, and progressed quickly enough to play in the Norwalk Symphony at age 12, and to win a scholarship to study in Fontainebleau, France, when I was 15. I guess the most memorable thing about that summer was the classes with Nadia Boulanger. Of course, I know much more about her now than I did then. I also studied horn with Jean Devemy of the Paris Conservatory there. Then the next year I won an Aetna Life Insurance scholarship for being the best high school musician in Connecticut. That was a very big deal for me at the time. Besides winning a thousand dollars, which was a lot of money in 1962, especially to a 16 year old, I got to play a guest appearance with the Hartford Symphony that was a live telecast. So by the time I finished high school I had definitely decided to become a professional musician.

How did your parents feel about that then?

David: Well, they were both proud and encouraging, but at the same time tried to caution me against a performing career, since the odds were pretty long against making any kind of substantial living at it. My father had wanted to be a performer, but ultimately went into teaching and found that he really loved it. And he's a very good teacher. But I've just always liked the thrill of performance. You don't get a second chance, you can't take your work home with you, and you're really only as good as your last performance. Even back then, I was driven by all of that, and learned early on how to handle the nerves pretty well.

How did you decide where to go after high school?

David: I had been very directed since my mid-teens, and had made up my mind that there was only one college that I wanted to apply to: the New England Conservatory. Luckily, I wound up getting a full scholarship. I knew exactly who I wanted to study with there because for years I had listened to the classical radio station from Boston, which was on in our house all day, and to tons of records in high school—you know, the Tchaikovsky Fifth and like that—and on my own decided that the horn player in the Boston Symphony was a great player. I wanted to know what he thought about to be able to play music like that! I guess I wanted to emulate him, and I found out where he taught and went there.

Who was he?

David: His name was James Stagliano—they called him the Stallion—and he was *quite* a personality in the Boston Symphony. He had joined in 1947 or something like that, and had been first horn there for over 25 years before he finally retired. I knew him the last 10 years or so of his career. He never had a son and always wanted one, so he kind of adopted me and took me under his wing. Jimmy taught me a lot of things: he taught me about the horn, he taught me about total concentration, he taught me about the actual hands-on experience of playing in an orchestra, and I guess you could also say that he taught me a lot about life in general. He had a good business sense, and even started his own record company for recording Boston Symphony artists called Boston Records. It was eventually bought by RCA. He just always had these things cooking. I spent a lot of time with Jimmy, and he was a good role model for me in some ways—in some ways not—but in many ways he was. When I went to college I could already play the horn, but I didn't know that much about music. His strength as a teacher was in teaching music, in things like showing me how to approach a phrase. He wasn't good at giving exercises and etudes. He was good at teaching the expressive stuff, the intangible of music. He used to say, "Look, all these guys come in and play a million notes in auditions, and yet they can't play one phrase or even one beautiful note that makes you cry." He stressed that with me, and I became very much in his mold in that way. And I'm sure that a couple of years later when I won the audition with the Chicago Symphony, it was because I was able to bring something beyond technique in a world that's always striving for technical perfection and speed and evenness and flawless intonation—all these things that are the external things of music, but not the internal essence of it. If you take away all the notes and rhythms and technique and speed, and all you've got is that little shining star that is left, what is it? Why did Mozart sit down at his paper and write those particular notes in that way? It certainly wasn't a technical exercise. What inspired him to do that? They say that music is the language that starts where words leave off, and that was it, I guess. Jimmy Stagliano helped me discover that language.

I want to get back to the Chicago audition, but first tell us a little more about your college days.

David: School was good. I spent an enormous amount of time in the practice room. And I started free-lancing in Boston while I was in college. I played with Sarah Caldwell and the Boston Opera Company, went on tours of different kinds, played for the ballet, played first horn in a chamber symphony, played in a brass quintet and a woodwind quintet—you know, just everything that free-lancers do. Most important for me was that I started playing extra with Boston Symphony about that time. So I had a full musical schedule, and it wasn't like you go to school and get out and then get a job. I was working all during my student days, so that when I graduated all of that free-lance work just continued. The only difference was that I wasn't in school anymore. Two and a half years after college was when I won the Chicago Symphony audition, and within a week of that offer I was offered a horn position in the Boston Symphony, since they happened to have an opening at that time and knew my playing. For a week there I had horn jobs in two of the best orchestras in the world! I was 24 years old and they were fighting over me. It was great.

How did you decide?

David: Believe it or not, it was pretty easy. You have to remember that I had grown up a New England boy. Boston had always been the place to be for me. Even in my high school yearbook under my senior picture it reads "Secret Ambition: Be in the Boston Symphony." It was the orchestra that I had grown up around. I went to Tanglewood for three summers as a student, and had been playing extra with them for five or six years. I had recorded big pieces with them like Mahler, Strauss and Wagner when they hired extra horn players. I was *right there*, you know? But I wasn't really part of the orchestra. So when they offered me a contract it was a personal thing, the fulfillment of a dream really. Even though many people might think that Chicago is the best brass section in the world, I still wanted very much to be in

David with the Empire Brass, c. 1981. Left to right, David, Charles Lewis, Sam Pilafian, Don Sanders, Rolf Smedvig.

Playing on the sidewalk, November 1990, at the opening of the Moscow McDonald's.

the Boston Symphony. And I'm not at all sorry for that decision. I had fantastic training in Boston for orchestra playing. I know all the literature now. I played under great conductors. I had a helluva good time as a member of that orchestra. I got to see China, Japan a few times, and Europe a bunch of times. So I have no regrets about it. I did it long enough so that I don't really miss it. I don't feel like "if I'd only gotten to play this piece or that piece." I got a chance to play all the big orchestra pieces I'd dreamed of playing since high school.

I wonder if people realize what orchestra players go through with blind auditions?

David: It's behind a screen. They never even see you. You could be 15 years old or 50 years old. You could be illiterate. You could! Sometimes it might help. *(laughs)* You're not allowed to speak at all; you just play what you're told. "Excerpt number 27, please," and you play that, then "Excerpt number 43." And then you play your concerto movement or whatever. You're just a number. It's kind of odd. People who aspire to be classical performers automatically go to music school and get a degree, or degrees in some cases. But when you play an audition they don't care if you have a degree at all. All they care about is the one narrow craft or discipline that you have, because that's what they've appealed for. Students sometimes ask me where they should go to college, and I really have no good answer for them. The school itself is not always that important. What is important is finding a teacher who can inspire you and be a role model for you as a musician, and can direct the talent and energy you have toward a positive goal. Maybe some talented kids who are performers aren't best suited to go to a traditional music school. I have a degree in performance, but if a university hires me later on down the road to teach when I'm too old to run around the world playing my horn, it probably won't be because of that degree. It will probably be because I've been in Canadian Brass and Empire Brass, and played in the Boston Symphony, and taught at Boston University for ten years.

When you were playing in the Boston Symphony did you also play with the Boston Pops?

David: Yes. Except for the principal players it's essentially the same orchestra that dresses in different clothes and plays different music for a different conductor. The contract that you sign is with the Boston Symphony, and that includes the Pops too.

So you performed under Arthur Fiedler, and did a lot of his...

David: Oh yeah. All the TV shows when he was at the height of his fame, and all the recordings. I got to know Fiedler personally, and he was quite a guy. Curmudgeonly old sort. He could turn on the charm, but basically he was kind of ... well, kind of a nasty guy. *(laughs)* He never seemed to be too interested in his family or the people around him. Conducting was his thing. His daughter and I were friends, so I got to see him occasionally away from the concert hall. One thing I remember about him was that he was really tight with a dollar! When I was a student I played in the Springfield Symphony, which is an hour or so from Boston. Every year Fiedler would come and conduct at Springfield in a pops concert where he could be a big star, and the orchestra would make a bunch of money. He did this kind of thing all over the country, of course. His manager in Boston found out that I drove a black Volkswagen, and for some strange reason that was Fiedler's car, eccentric that he was. Every year he'd buy a brand new black Volkswagen. I guess he only felt comfortable riding in that particular car. Anyway, his manager called me and said, "I know you're playing in Springfield. Would you give the maestro a ride out for the series?" It meant out and back for the rehearsal one night, and making the trip again for the concert the next night. Now, here's a guy who was worth millions, right? He could have hired a limo or even a helicopter and written it off on his taxes, no problem. But there I was in my black Beetle, pulling up to this gigantic mansion of a house! He had a very set procedure for the expenses of the trip: *(he pauses, as if setting up a punchline)* I paid the gas and he paid the tolls. Amazing? *(laughing)* I thought, O.K., well, it's better than nothing. That was Arthur. But he was a good conductor. He had a very good ear, and was able to get a brass sound that was very energetic and perky. He did it almost entirely with the stick. He always did basically the same concert. His repertory was very set, so you knew these pieces cold. He always had his own set of parts, and all through them would be Fiedler's comments written in by some anonymous player from years before. It would be a little message like "he's going to tell you to play this note short." And sure enough, in the rehearsal when you got to that spot Fiedler would stop and ask you to play the note staccato. His routine was so exactly set that each time he would say exactly the same things.

You played in Boston for ten years?

David: A little more than that, from 1970 to 1981. Then in 1981 I left along with trumpet player Rolf Smedvig to do Empire Brass. I'll have to back up a bit to pick up that story. We started rehearsing Empire in 1972. At that time I was in the Boston Symphony, but none of the other fellows were. Then in 1974 Rolf joined the Symphony, and in 1975 or 1976 trombonist Norm Bolter also joined the Symphony. So at that point three of the Empire Brass members were playing in the Boston Symphony, and people thought that the quintet was an outgrowth from that orchestra, when actually we had been together years before that. We kept rehearsing and performing as much as we could, commissioning pieces along the way. At that point the best we could do was to battle out of the orchestra's schedule for a two or three week tour every year. All that time we were watching Canadian Brass, and we knew that they were out there creating a market for brass groups. We believed in that too, and wanted a part of that action for ourselves. Then in 1976 we won the Naumburg prize, which was the first time a brass group had ever won the chamber music division of that competition. Things started happening for us. We got a record contract with CBS, and for the bicentennial we recorded traditional American brass music that we had rediscovered in the Library of Congress. I remember that we played for Jimmy Carter's inauguration about that time. So all of this kind of put us on the map. We made some more records, and although all five of us had other commitments, Empire Brass was really our first love, and we were putting a great deal of energy and effort into it.

Then in 1981 you decided to leave Boston Symphony to do Empire Brass full time?

Rehearsals for the triple quintet Gabrieli-Monteverdi fest at St. John the Divine, New York City, 1989. *Above:* Horn talk with Phil Myers of the New York Philharmonic.

Where is everybody? I thought rehearsals started at 7 a.m. today.

David: Rolf and I left the Symphony at the same time. Norm Bolter decided that he wanted to stay, and he's still there as a matter of fact. So we got another trombone player and went out on the road and did ninety concerts that first year with Columbia Artists as our management. My daughter had been born in December of 1979, so we had a young child at home, and it was a big change for me and my wife for me to be traveling so much. But it was just something that I had to do. Luckily my wife was a good sport and adaptable enough to go along with it. We were doing a lot of hard work with Empire Brass for very short money in the early '80s at a time when Canadian Brass was quite prominent. Without a doubt they had emerged as the premiere brass quintet in the world. And not just the premiere brass quintet. To say that sounds like everybody is kind of doing the same thing. They had a unique idea and a distinctive approach to the whole concert experience. It was to draw the audience into what they were doing, as opposed to just giving a traditional offering of music. I saw all this from afar. I was very aware of the group, and would buy their records, but I never had the chance to see them live until 1982 or 1983 when they played with the Boston Pops. It's worth mentioning that since Canadian Brass was a good four or five years ahead of us in the marketplace, they were continually creating a new plateau of fee structure. So when they were successful in raising their fees, then we would be able to raise ours too, keeping pace a notch below them. And the other brass groups down the ladder would be able to raise their fees as a result.

That ripple effect must have benefited lots of brass players.

David: Oh, absolutely. One of the great contributions of Canadian Brass is that they have really spearheaded a whole new concert industry for brass players. Brass quintets have been around since at least the 1950s, but nobody knew what to do with them for a long time. They were playing the same instruments that we are, 2 trumpets, horn, trombone and tuba, but just basically sat around in a circle and played more for themselves than anyone else. Since Canadian Brass proved that popular success is possible with a classical brass ensemble, there are unprecedented opportunities that have opened up for brass players. Any record store you walk into now has a bin for Canadian Brass recordings, and you always see recordings by other brass groups as well. That certainly wasn't true fifteen years ago. Turn on a classical music station and at some time during the day you're going to hear brass chamber music. Every concert series in North America books brass quintets now. Concert managers will tell you that brass groups are the fastest growing area of classical concerts these days. Twenty years ago none of this existed, and it all would have seemed far-fetched had anyone suggested it then. And Canadian Brass deserves most of the credit for all this. They succeeded so well in creating an audience for brass music that sometimes when I was still with Empire Brass people would say, "Gee, you guys really played great, but we kind of expected a show like Canadian Brass." Like now they expect that every brass group is going to be a Canadian Brass act!

That must have been a lot of fun to hear at the time!

David: Yeah. Sure. *(laughing)*

The transition for you from Empire Brass to Canadian Brass came in 1986?

David: By 1986 Empire Brass was doing very well. We had a bunch of records out, and it was pretty clear that we were the number two brass quintet in the business. Canadian Brass had a horn opening, and it was logical for them to look to me. Actually, they called to ask me if I could recommend anyone. At first I didn't really see the opportunity that was there for me. I was still very much on the team of Empire Brass, and I wanted to continue to realize the dream that I had had as one of the founders of that group, and reap the rewards of all the years of hard work I had put into it. But the more I thought about it, the more I realized that this change would be an advantage for me in just about every way. The disadvantages would only be in the short term—the inconvenience of selling a house and buying another house, moving to a different country, uprooting our daughter from school, and leaving all my friends. I'd lived in Boston for twenty-three years, but I began to realize that there were a lot of roots there that would not be impossible to pull up. When I got to that

above: Tanglewood, 1989; Charles Schlueter of the Boston Symphony, Phil Smith of the New York Philharmonic, Fred, and Mark Gould of the Metropolitan Opera Orchestra in front of David and his favorite Maserati from his car collection

below: rehearsal—anytime, anywhere

point in my thinking it was just kind of a laziness that was holding me back for a little while. But as soon as I made up my mind it was a relatively easy transition. Thank goodness that, for whatever reason, I'm blessed with a good musical memory, so learning a whole new repertory was not as hard on me as it might have been for someone else. A lot of what we do in Canadian Brass is memorized, and a good chunk of it is choreographed. So when I went up to Toronto to cement the deal I walked away with a pile of music, a pile of recordings, and several video tapes. And from that day I had exactly one month before I began my first tour with Canadian Brass.

That must have been kind of overwhelming.

David: Actually, it was a fun month. The first thing I did was to sit down and learn all the music, and memorized what needed to be memorized. Then I would put on their recordings and play along to get a feel for how they did the pieces. To learn the choreography I'd put on the video tapes and look over my shoulder while I learned the steps. I went up to Toronto for a week of rehearsals with the guys, and then we got on a plane to do a tour of the Far East. So my first concerts with Canadian Brass were in Singapore, Hong Kong and Japan. I definitely hit the ground running, but it was exciting to be doing something brand new with new people in far away places. Besides the sheer fun of it, I realized that I was the one person in the whole world best suited to become a part of this very well established ensemble. Suddenly, the logical progression of my career up to that point all made sense to me in a new way.

What are your thoughts when you look back on it all?

David: Tremendous satisfaction. And a tremendous feeling that good fortune has come my way. I know talented players who have had dreams of really reaching the top of the music profession and didn't, and are playing today in third and fourth line orchestras and selling shoes to make enough money to get by. I'm sure I could learn some things from them. I mean, everybody has strengths and weaknesses. I guess ... *(his voice softens and his conversation becomes slower)* ... I guess I like to think that my dedication and talent and all the years of hard work and the sacrifices I've made mean that I deserve all the good things in my life and that I've earned every bit of it. But I know that luck played a great part. Maybe even the greatest part. I know I'm a lucky person! I'm *very lucky*. But I don't know...it just seems more than coincidence that I was in the right place at the right time so often. It seems more than coincidence that Jimmy Stagliano just happened to have taken me under his wing and invested so much of himself in me and annoyed me and pushed me and gave me so many opportunities. It seems more than coincidence that I won that audition in Chicago and got the offer from Boston at the same time. I was 24 years old and everybody in the orchestra world knew my name. I had hit the business a hit. It seems more than coincidence that in 1981 I began to devote a full time career to playing in a brass quintet, which had been a longtime wish of mine. I had overwhelming advice from my wife, my father, my friends and colleagues to remain in the Boston Symphony, but I knew within myself that the timing was right to make a move. And it seems more than coincidence that Canadian Brass called me, too. It's just that there's some pattern to it all. If you try to look back on it your emotions can get very tangled, and you say to yourself, "Well, maybe it would have all worked out the same if I hadn't worked at it, and if I had just let it happen." But then again, you can never really be quite sure about that. *(laughs)* So you just do what you have to do and hope that it adds up. I've had some disappointments along the way. I was very disappointed when I auditioned for first horn in the Boston Symphony and didn't get it. It was down to two of us, and I lost. But if I had become first horn there, I probably never would have left the Boston Symphony to do Empire Brass full time. Going back even further, if I had taken the job in Chicago then I never would have gotten together with those guys in Boston and formed Empire Brass in the first place. And then there would have been no particular reason for Canadian Brass to have called me. Gee—isn't life amazing?

Perched on the Great Wall of China.

R O N   R O M M

Did you come from a musical family?

Ron: *(he is soft-spoken, with a cheerful manner to all his conversation)*
Yes. My mother was a clarinetist who later also played the
saxophone. We had a family dance band, the Romm-Antics. So I
was around music from the time I was born. Usually it was pop
music of the 40s and 50s, but there was a good bit of classical
music around too. My father's father had immigrated to the
United States from Russia early in the century, and he loved
opera. He was part of a paid claque at the Metropolitan Opera at
one time. He went to the opera all the time anyway, so he used to
earn a few extra dollars for just cheering or booing as directed.
He knew all the operas, of course, and as a result we had all these
very interesting records at home. My parents had varied tastes as
well, so music around our house was very eclectic.

When did you begin taking lessons of some kind?

Ron: Well, I started on the piano when I was just about 7 years
old, and I have to say that I was not exactly Horowitz. As a
matter of fact, later when I was at Juilliard everyone had to take a
piano minor and pass a proficiency test in piano. They passed me
only because they never wanted to see my face again! That's the
truth! *(laughs)* So you can see that I never exactly progressed
very far on the piano, even many years after I'd started. But the
piano was somehow vaguely connected to my becoming a
trumpet player. We had this piano tuner who used to come to our
house—a very friendly old gentleman—and one day when I was
about 8 he looked at me and said, "I think you'd make a
wonderful cornetist." So we went to his music shop, and I tried
blowing into this cornet. There was no sound. At all. I just
couldn't make it work. Maybe I was a little too young. Anyway,
that must have planted a seed of interest, because about a year
later I had this burning desire to try it again. So I started on
trumpet when I was 9.

Trumpet, rather than cornet?

Ron: Cornet was not as popular for kids in Los Angeles, where I grew up, as it was in the midwest or the east. They're very different animals—they really are. The cornet is by nature gentler, and the trumpet tends to be a more aggressive instrument.

Do you think that being in Los Angeles had any special influence on you?

Ron: Of course, being in L.A. tends to put you in the mainstream of what we call "the business." My family band, which I began to play in as soon as I could, did live radio shows and television shows. I remember that when I was a kid we played the opening of the Satellite Five Western Airlines Satellite at LAX. I guess I remember that because Tony Randall was there. I wound up doing lots of performing and auditioning as a kid. I auditioned for "The Mickey Mouse Club" and "The Lawrence Welk Show"—lots of that kind of thing. I became proficient on the trumpet very quickly, and was a decent soloist pretty young. I played with the family band and lots of other places as a kid. That meant school music for me as well. The junior high school I went to, Orville Wright Junior High, had a very active band and orchestra program with something like ninety in the band and sixty-five in the orchestra. By the time people get to high school they usually move on to other interests that are different from those of their younger childhood. But I stayed with music. To tell the truth, I really wanted to be a veterinarian more than anything else. I've always had a great affinity for animals, and they seem to like me too. *(laughs)* I'm still a great one for roaming around the zoo with my kids whenever I can. Anyway, I stayed with music in hopes of getting a scholarship to finance my way through college to become a vet. And it's a good thing I did, because as it turned out I wasn't good enough in math to get into a pre-med program in college, which was a requisite at the time. So I just ended up staying with music all the way. At Westchester High I played in the band and orchestra. During the summers in high school I had been accepted into a special band program at USC. William A. Schaefer was the director—he's still there, by the way. I played there a couple of summers. Ingolf Dahl was around, and

above: The Romm-Antics, 1965, with Ron on trumpet, mother Sylvia on clarinet, father Sam on drums, and sister Eileen on piano.

below left: From a brochure for the Los Angeles Brass Quintet in Ron's USC days

1. Tom Stevens, trumpet
2. Ronald Romm, trumpet
3. Wayne Barrington, horn
4. Miles Anderson, trombone
5. Roger Bobo, tuba

Quintet

I was studying with Lester Remsen who was a principal trumpet teacher at USC. I played in the Collegium Musicum there too. My dad would drive me back and forth there for rehearsals and the classes, and we did basic theory, sight-singing and ear training. I know other musicians hate classes like that, but I thought it was really fun. I had Alice Ehler's class then—Michael Tilson Thomas studied harpsichord and early music with her. She was a great keyboard artist and teacher. Really terrific! So musically I had a good foundation before I went to college.

And all this time you continued playing with the family band?

Ron: That and lots of other things. I had been working as a professional player from the time I was 12 years old, and that has never stopped, thank goodness. When it came time to go to college I didn't have great grades in high school, but I was a pretty good trumpet player. I prepared an audition for USC, and got accepted with a good scholarship. I went there two years. While I was in school I was also playing with the Los Angeles Philharmonic. One of the trumpet players had suddenly passed away, and so there was kind of an urgent opening. I had auditioned for third trumpet and came in second, so that gave me first call on everything. I was fourth chair and the utility position, which was actually the most varied of the trumpet duties. I played for lots of things with them, even at the Hollywood Bowl. It also allowed me to play outside jobs when there was time. I played for other groups that toured into town—first trumpet in the pit for the Royal Ballet and groups like that. It was pretty heady stuff for a teenager to be doing! Then a year later the Philharmonic was required by law to have official auditions for that trumpet spot that had been vacated. I tied with Mario Guarnieri. It was during the Vietnam War and I was draft eligible. Mario was in the reserves, which made him draft-exempt. So rather than having a play-off, they took the safest route and hired him. That way I guess they figured that they could still use me as an extra player. Then things took a peculiar turn. My grades were slipping. I'd also fallen in love with a girl, and that ended, and I kind of crashed. You can probably tell from seeing me on stage that I wear my emotions on my sleeve. Anyway, it was a difficult time for me. I was almost drafted—they were taking people with flat feet and congenital heart disease—but I flunked the physical for the army, so at least that was out of the way. I decided to pack up and move to New York to go to Juilliard.

Did you know anyone in New York then?

Ron: I had made a few friends who were there. I rented a room from the parents of a friend's fiancé, and I stayed there the first couple of months because there was a foul-up with my transcripts and I couldn't get into school. In the middle of that idle semester the L.A. Philharmonic went on a cross-country tour and hired me to play with them. So I went back to Los Angeles, and wound up coming back to New York on tour with the Philharmonic, then back to L.A. with them again. It was kind of crazy. When I got back to New York after the tour I auditioned at Juilliard and luckily got a really good scholarship. When I got there Gerard Schwartz was playing in the first orchestra. They had room for me in the reading orchestra, which was really fun. All the student conductors worked with that group, and we would teach them some things as well as learn from them. There was a nice interchange of ideas and and a wonderful creative environment. It was refreshing to work with conductors who weren't invincible yet. *(laughs)*

What were classes like there?

Ron: I was taking ear-training from Madame Longy, who had once flunked Leonard Bernstein because he wasn't working up to his capacity! She was one tough teacher. We had to play three clefs simultaneously and sing a fourth. She took pity on me and my non-pianistic abilities and only made me play two clefs at a time and sing a third. And all the while she would slam her hand thunderously on the desk to keep time. In that class I met this wonderful young lady—a very pretty, charming, shy girl who sat next to me. I don't know why, but I kept forgetting her name. She was great in that class, and could play piano very well, could read a full score, and do as many clefs as she had fingers. I finally got her name straight and we became friends, and eventually got married. I guess in the back of my mind I figured that since I

77

left:
With Timofey
Dokshitzer,
Russia's
foremost
trumpet
virtuoso

below:
On the stage
of Carnegie
Hall, 1985;
William
Vacchiano
(rear right)
with four star
students
Carmine
Fornarotto,
Phil Smith,
Ron and Fred

couldn't play the piano I'd better marry someone who could! *(laughs)* We've been married more than twenty years now. Avis is a wonderful musician, an intuitive pianist and a superb vocal coach. She knows all the operatic repertory backwards and forwards.

When you were at Juilliard did you continue free-lancing?

Ron: Yeah, I was running around doing everything, essentially working full-time and going to school full-time too. I played regularly at Radio City Music Hall, and with lots of other groups. One job I remember fondly was doing Monteverdi's *Orfeo* with Charlotte Bergen at Town Hall, something that she did as an annual event. *Orfeo* was her passion. There were nine trumpets and some sackbuts in the orchestra. I played absolutely everything and everywhere in those years, and sometimes played with Fred on jobs, because he was also in New York at the time. I subbed in shows on Broadway, which was kind of fun. I remember playing in the pit for the Stephen Sondheim show *Company*. Once I was doing the Music Hall and the ice show at the same time, and in the space of one day I'd have to play the ice show, which was very long, and two shows at the Music Hall. My lips were sticking out about six inches by the time I was done! *(laughs)* In the middle of all this I was playing in a brass quintet that rehearsed four nights a week from 11 p.m. till about 2 in the morning, if you can believe that. The crazy things we do when we're young! I somehow got out of Juilliard with a master's degree, even though I was being pulled in ten directions constantly with the free-lancing. Avis finished school a year ahead of me and was playing all kinds of free-lance work herself then.

When did you join Canadian Brass?

Ron: Fred and I had stayed in contact after he moved back to Canada. Soon after I finished school he called from Ottawa one day to say, "This brass quintet they're trying to get off the ground in Toronto has an opening. One of the guys is leaving and going back to school. Why don't you play for them?" It was right at that time that Canadian Brass, which had just gotten going, was moving from Toronto to Hamilton to be in residence with the Hamilton Philharmonic and to do this innovative educational program there. Gene had already bought a house in Hamilton, and I played a casual audition there with them. They auditioned me, and I auditioned them too. It was a beautiful, sunny day and everything seemed right about it. I liked the other guys right away. Avis and I were really tired of New York, and the thought of moving to this small Canadian city was very refreshing. So we moved there and I began with Canadian Brass. Getting Fred in the group was a great plus for me. We had always gotten along very well, and had already played together quite a bit in New York and at the National Ballet of Canada Orchestra. We work well as a section, and are both versatile and can rely on one another, which is very important for the trumpets in a brass quintet.

You do a fair amount of solo work in the group's repertory.

Ron: I'm a decent soloist, I guess. *(Ron is being characteristically modest.)* I just try to keep the music alive. I enjoy the solo work, but I enjoy the ensemble work just as much. I was lucky to find a group like Canadian Brass, where everyone is really a soloist—and an accompanist, and a music director, a manager, and a travel agent. We all do so many things at the same time.

What's hardest for you about touring?

Ron: I don't always sleep regularly. It used to bother me a lot, but now I've learned to go along with it and catch it later if it doesn't come easily. But sometimes I get pretty beaten down toward the end of a tour. Of course, I have to fit into the regular rehearsal and travel schedule with everyone, even though my waking-sleeping cycle isn't always a normal one.

With the kind of travel schedule you have, how have you stayed married all these years?

Ron: Avis has always been nice enough to adapt and go with my schedule. It's nice to come off the road and have someone there who is looking forward to seeing you. She's fantastic and is able to handle absolutely everything. I really don't know how she does it! She and the kids run the house perfectly well when I'm not there, and they get along fine without me. They say they don't, but I know better! *(laughs)* In a career like this it's always been impossible for me to leave the business at the office so to speak. I tend to bring everything home with me from the stage or recording studio or rehearsal hall. So my state of mind always reflects how things are going for the quintet. Avis has this great ability to be steady and keep me on an even keel.

How old are your children?

Ron: We have two boys, an 11-year-old, Orlan, and a 7-year-old, Aaron. They're such a delight to me. Both of them seem to have perfect pitch. They'll be singing a song they like, and I'll try going over to the piano to play the tune, and they're always in the right key. The older one used to sing all the time, but now that he's in school he doesn't sing as much anymore. The little one sings all day long. Sometimes I try and imagine what the world will be like for them when they grow up, and it's mind boggling. During my father's lifetime he saw the horse and buggy, the automobile, airplanes and spacecrafts—just an enormous amount of fast and constant change. And things continue to change at a faster pace all the time. I recently read that sixty per cent of the children born today will be pursuing professional careers that don't even exist now! It staggers the imagination.

Do your children ever come to see you perform?

Ron: Once in awhile they come and see me in concert, particularly in Florida, where we live now. They see me on television, and watch the videos and play the records and sing along. They're very much aware of what Dad does, and they seem to enjoy it, except that they tell me that I'm away too much. It's hard for all of us.

I believe that you spend some of your free time flying, don't you?

Ron: I got interested in flying in 1979. About that time the

above: Two activities, in addition to flying, that are less dangerous than performing for a living— skiing ("It was my first and only time on skis, and this was definitely the 'before' picture") and motor-cycling (with Avis at Banff, 1977)

right: The Romms, with Orlan (left) and Aaron

Canadian Brass started chartering small planes occasionally. I'd sit in the right seat up front, next to the pilot, and I guess I really caught the flying bug. I went in and took the examinations, took some lessons, and got involved right away. I bought a plane a couple of years after I started flying, and I still have that. It's a Robin Sport, a French design, and can do some aerobatics. What I like best is that it has a bubble canopy, which is really great for sight-seeing. When I'm flying it's a complete escape. You're totally set free. There are no telephones, no one to bother me—I can't even bother myself. I can simply think about flying and the task at hand. Usually when I'm home, when the weather's good, I'll fly two or three times a week. And when the weather's not good I might just go down to the airport and wash the plane, or hang out with the guys down there. I've flown to jobs once in awhile, but I've found that I'd much rather use the plane for pure pleasure. If I were to fly to a concert, I'd have to worry about getting there on time, and that's tough to do with a small plane. It would create stress that I just don't need.

One thing that I'm sure many brass players would like to ask you is if there is a limit to how much you can play in a day?

Ron: I think that we're still trying to find that limit. It may be that as we get older as players we may tire more easily physically, but we're also a little craftier, so that we can pace ourselves better in a way that isn't very detectable to a listener. It's not that you're slacking off or playing lazy, but when you play as much as we do you can find ways to coast a bit sometimes. We've long since been able to play two full concerts in one day, and have on occasion even played three appearances in one day.

When you have to perform that much in a day, do you warm up less?

Ron: Not at all. No, in fact, you warm up more. It's really an athletic endeavor, and so you have to prepare for it. If you know you're going to have to perform for a total of three hours on a given day, you warm up enough so that you get it flowing as easily as possible, and that can take some time. But I do have to admit that by the end of two concerts you begin to really feel fatigue, both mentally and physically.

above:
Ron shows his
plane to Fred and
Philip Jones
left:
Ron and Fred
with an ecstatic
Les Brown
below:
With Jack
Sheldon

One of the eternal questions always asked about the trumpets in a brass quintet is who plays first trumpet and who plays second?

Ron: Well, in our case, instead of one person playing first and one playing second, it's really a double play combination, to spin it into baseball lingo. Each of us does certain things well, and for each piece we sort out the parts based on what's required. Fred has a wonderful light touch and ability to play with incredibly crisp articulation and clarity. My playing is naturally a bigger sound with a little more color. It's the difference between two talented painters, one who best uses an intricate, detailed brush stroke, and the other who's at his best using bigger, broader strokes. We also constantly are changing our minds about what instrument to play a part on, be it a piccolo trumpet, or an E flat trumpet, or B flat or whatever. We rehearse a good deal, and usually in rehearsal I'll have plenty of opportunity to experiment with different instruments. But even on a piece we've been playing for a couple of years, one day I might decide to try the part on another instrument. We're always working on new material for recordings, and the more we play it, the better a feel we get for how it should sound, and what instrument to play it on. I know it's probably hard for some people to understand, but it seems that the longer the group is together, the more we rehearse. Part of that is because our record contract is now for two albums a year. Just working up that much new material takes time. But also I think that we've learned the value of playing a piece many times for it to congeal in a way that feels absolutely comfortable for everyone. It's not really a matter of getting the notes, because we get the notes right pretty quickly. It's more a matter of making the piece feel like a familiar old friend that you know so well that it becomes second nature. That takes time. I guess that what it really means is that the better we get, if you want to think of it that way, the higher our standards are. But it's not something that we've necessarily had to consciously foster. It's grown naturally out of what we've done in the past and what we bring to any new piece.

It's pretty remarkable that the group has stayed together so long and so successfully.

Ron: I think that we've continued on a high-growth pace because we're able to restore our energies rather than burn them out. We can function at a high level of activity constantly and repeatedly. I believe that most groups wouldn't be able to keep the kind of schedule we keep without feeling severe adverse effects. But we have found a way of staying on top of it by respecting one another and by being careful to continually restore our mental and physical energies and focus them toward a common creative goal. To some extent being in the Brass is like group therapy. We've known one another so long that nobody lets you get away with much. You're constantly being kept in perspective as an individual by the other members.

One last question. Do you have a favorite album that you've recorded with the Brass?

Ron: Hey, every one of those albums is still in print, and there are copies in record stores everywhere. So if you want my absolutely candid answer, I guess I'd have to say they're all my favorites! *(laughs)*

GENE WATTS

Where did you grow up?

Gene: *(he is very animated as he talks, with large, enthusiastic gestures)* I was born in Warrensburg, Missouri, but my first memories are of Lincoln, Missouri. Then when I was still a kid we moved to the much larger metropolis of Sedalia, Missouri. So you can see that I had a very cosmopolitan childhood.

How did music start for you?

Gene: My mother was a piano teacher, and she would finish giving lessons for the day and I'd go to the piano and play exactly the same music as I had just heard the other kids play. Just like Mozart, right? Well, maybe not. My mother and my brother would laugh at this, because even though to my little pre-school ears the music sounded right, apparently it was just a bunch of noise and didn't resemble anything at all. After that I never could play the piano!

Was there brass music in your home?

Gene: My brother played trumpet, and my father used to play trumpet as well. My father's childhood is quite a story in itself. He grew up in in Arkansas, and his mother was a lay preacher. She would take him around to all the churches where she preached, and because some of these country churches had no piano or organ, he would lead the hymns on the trumpet or violin. He also started preaching himself at something like age 12. So I guess you could say that I have show business roots of a sort. Anyway, since my brother played trumpet, I wanted to play trumpet too. Then about that time an instrument salesman came around to our house in Sedalia and said my lips were too big to play trumpet, but that he had a nice euphonium that he thought would be just right for me. So we fell for that. Hey, what did we

top left: Father J.W., mother Nora, brother Jim and little Gene. *top right:* Age 13. *bottom:* The Missouri Mudcats— Gene's college tuition paid in Saturday night installments, with Bob James on piano

know? I got this euphonium, which seemed gargantuan at first to me, and played that for a while. But at the time I wanted most to play dance music and jazz, and switched to trombone. I started my own dance band in my teens, and also worked in a music store then. Sedalia is kind of an interesting town because during the 19th century it was more or less the end of the underground railroad in that region for slaves escaping from the South. All those Missouri towns in that area had a highly active musical life in the black section of town. After all, Sedalia was the home town of Scott Joplin, so there was a musical tradition there. Musicians would travel from town to town, and when I was in high school I started hearing the jazz players who'd come to town. So when I had started my own band I would hire some of these players to play with us. They were a tremendous musical influence on me. Then I went to the University of Missouri in Columbia and had my own band there all through college, a Dixieland band called the Missouri Mudcats. It actually paid for my entire education there. About that time I got married and decided that I should probably look for something more stable than playing in a Dixieland band. So I went into classical music. *(laughs)* I looked around, and wound up at the New England Conservatory in Boston. I studied there three years, and then got a job with the North Carolina Symphony, followed by a stay in the San Antonio Symphony, which was followed by couple of years in the Milwaukee Symphony. There were other things along the way, like studying with Arnold Jacobs in Chicago in the summers and selling shoes. Jake was a very important influence on me, as was Schilke.

Those two men seem to have been important influences on a legion of musicians.

Gene: Well, they certainly were giants to me. And I have some colorful memories of them. My brother was attending Northwestern and living with Ren Schilke, so I went there in the summers to work and study music. That's where I heard Schilke and the Chicago Brass Quintet rehearsing every Sunday. When I left to go back to Missouri I owed him $100 for lessons. He told me if I practiced and worked real hard, I wouldn't have to pay him. I also worked for him, painting music stands, and helping him out in little ways. Once I dropped a whole tray of buffed new mouthpieces! After that was when I started painting music stands. He never had me carry mouthpieces again. *(laughs)* Studies with Arnold Jacob came two years later. I had left college to go on the road with the territory bands out of Lincoln, Nebraska—you know, dance bands. After about 4 months on the road I decided to go back to Chicago, and that's when I started studying with Jacobs. At the time I was also playing in a small club in Calumet City. In those days Calumet City was run by the syndicate. One night my car was parked outside of the club, and some drunken driver banged into it. It turned out that he was underage and had been drinking in the clubs. The policeman asked me if I wanted to press charges, and of course I said yes. The next day the insurance company contacted me and said they would pay me for the damages if I wouldn't press charges. Since the driver was underage, if charges were pressed, they'd have to close the club. As it turned out, they paid me so much money that I was able to fix the car and go back to school at Columbia.

When I was in the Milwaukee Symphony a few years later I was able to spend more time studying with Jake. He's like a musical psychiatrist. He has wonderful ways of approaching problems in playing an instrument. Most all problems are found in a player's breathing. He attacks problems by not looking at the results, but the cause. In other words, if you have tonguing problems, he doesn't work on the actual tonguing, but would go the the root of the problem—the breath. He has the wonderful ability to help a person have the experience of playing properly and naturally. He's constantly stressing that what you're doing isn't a technical exercise—you're making music. But in order to do that your technique must free you.

How did you wind up in Toronto?

Gene: I was playing in Tanglewood and Seiji Ozawa was there holding auditions for the Toronto Symphony, where he had just become conductor. I won that audition and played in Toronto with the symphony for three years. Looking back on it, I don't think I was temperamentally cut out to be an orchestra player. You really have to focus only on playing your own part, and must

above left: He's not sure where, but guesses Nome, Alaska
above right: Bangkok, 1981
below: Looking inspired at Radio Italiana, Venice, 1976

forget about everything else going on in the orchestra. I never was able to do that. I had too many ideas and reactions to whatever was going on. But going the orchestra route was worthwhile for a few years. I did learn a lot from those jobs, particularly playing under Ozawa. The last year with the Toronto Symphony was when I started meditating.

By that you mean Transcendental Meditation?

Gene: That's right. I started meditating, and after about six or seven months I began to realize that it was more valuable to me than I realized. After I left the orchestra job in Toronto I decided to go to India for a while and study meditation. You have to remember that this was the late '60s, and this kind of adventure was part of climate of that time. So I applied, was accepted, and went to India for three months. I was very curious about what study with the Maharishi really meant. I was a little worried that it might be Hinduism, or some other kind of "ism" that didn't really apply to me. What I found was that it's basically a search for self-knowledge, which for me fit into everything I had learned in a Christian upbringing, but in a new and vital way. I think I started to see who I was as a person and a musician, and to see what were my natural abilities and inclinations. I really think that the whole experience in India got me in a frame of mind to come back to Toronto and begin the Canadian Brass.

Do the other guys in the group also meditate?

Gene: Yes. Part of my study in India was about instructing others in meditation, and so I taught the other guys. Actually, Freddy and I started TM at about the same time.

Do you think that meditation has anything to do with the group's success?

Gene: I do see a connection. How do you communicate to an audience anyway? You do it through speech, music, or acting, but how well you communicate really depends on the level of consciousness in each performer. This is difficult to talk about because we really don't have accurate words for it. Meditation is about finding the level of silence inside yourself. A performer has a difficult time finding any inner silence. I mean, you get up in front of an audience and you can become distracted by a million neurotic thoughts running into your head. "Am I going to be able to play this? Will I remember all the details from the last rehearsal? Do they like me? Why isn't the theatre full? Is my fly open?" You know, just a barrage of self-conscious thoughts. Actually, what happens is that you become much more aware of yourself on stage. That's why people get hooked on performing. It greatly heightens awareness of yourself. That's the same thing that happens in meditation. You close your eyes, and suddenly you're aware of all your thoughts. Your sensitivity and awareness of yourself is strengthened. The stronger a person is, the more silence and peace he can find. He walks into a room, and rather than projecting tension or depression or insecurity or whatever, his inner peace affects the whole room. So when a performer walks on stage, his level of silence is reflected to the audience. In other words, the performer takes the audience to his level. If the audience is taken closer to "bliss," for lack of a better word, then the performance is thrilling and enjoyable. The really exciting thing is that if the audience is taken to a common, positive state of being, and they are projecting that energy back onto the stage, then the performer can achieve a much deeper level of "silence" than is normally attainable. If your nerves are strong and you can handle it, it will feed you and the situation in a profound way. If you can't handle it, then you'll become tense and won't be able to go with the flow. I think that anyone who has performed in front of an audience can perhaps understand a little of what I mean, even if they know nothing about meditation. Now, uh ...where were we?

You had left the Toronto Symphony and gone to India for three months.

Gene: How could I forget? Although the symphony job in Toronto didn't work out, I liked the city very much, had made a lot of friends and connections there, and decided to stay. I started playing lots of new music on contemporary concerts. I think my jazz background combined with the classical training allowed me to be a little freer to play a lot of improvisation and non-traditional things that were required for playing contemporary music in those days. I naturally became interested in starting an ensemble myself. I'd always wanted very much to start a brass quintet, and felt that it was how I could best express my talents as a musician and a person. When I started the quintet it wasn't just something to do for fun. Actually, it's kind of misleading to say that I started the Canadian Brass, because I really feel that the whole thing didn't come together until we had the right mix of people. We had been rehearsing with this other tuba player for a little while, but then Chuck played with us and we realized that he was what we needed. There was an exciting chemistry with him that was apparent right away. He's going to hate me for telling this story, but when we signed in Hamilton it was for $12,000 each per year, which was big money back then for that orchestra. Chuck came onto the scene, and he had just graduated from Eastman and was teaching at the University of Toronto at the time. He was filling in with the orchestra some, and we asked him what he was making. Chuck very proudly said "$15 a session." After we recovered from our squelched laughter, the first thing we did was start negotiating for him for better pay. And to think that now he's one of the toughest wheeler-dealers around. *(laughs)* Actually, it was quite a task to convince the management at Hamilton that the orchestra, which was really a chamber orchestra, needed a full-time tuba! But we went in and said, "We gotta have Chuck because he's got a Ph. D. in music education and everything, and here we're going to be doing all this work with the schools." And basically we used whatever logic we could, just because we knew that Chuck was the guy that we needed to complete the quintet. Thank goodness they fell for it. But I do believe that he was the first full-time tuba player ever in a chamber orchestra in the history of chamber orchestras! Chuck has tremendous energy and drive. He has a unquenchable need to be in front of an audience and express himself publicly. His personality and drive is essential to what has built the group. Any act has to have that kind of steady source of energy and drive that's necessary to keep moving forward.

In considering the career of the Canadian Brass, the group has always seemed to move forward, from the early days in Hamilton, until today.

 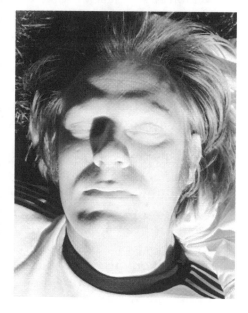

top: No comment
bottom left: He's still strying to play the piano
bottom right: An action shot of Gene meditating

Gene: I think that whatever the performing situation over the years, we've always respected it, whether it be playing for school children or at Carnegie Hall. That might be one reason we've continued to achieve. It's that old idea that if you make the present as rich as you can, then the future will take care of itself. Concerning audiences, our philosophy has always been to try to let the audience go away happy, and glad that we had played for them. People sometimes say to us, "Don't you guys get bored playing 'Little Fugue in G minor' after 20 years?" What they don't understand is when you continue to connect with an audience with that piece, and have positive reactions from them when you play that music, how could you ever become bored? It's not important to prove how good you are to an audience, or how many pieces you can learn. What's important is connecting—the relationship to the listeners. That seems very simple, but I'm not sure that musicians have really accepted that. In our universities and studios we know how to technically train good musicians. You can even coach someone to create a musical performance. But we don't really teach people what it means to perform.

Do you come up with most of the Brass' programming ideas?

Gene: Yes and no. I come up with most of the ideas, but the other guys have their input and reactions, and although I might shape the direction of what we're doing, we wind up deciding together about repertory. We all have a role to play in the life of the group, beyond what goes on when we're performing. I'm always especially interested in constantly thinking about what our next album should be, and try to develop concepts for recordings. People don't realize perhaps that, unlike most other classical ensembles, we've had to create everything we do from scratch. There has been no large body of brass quintet literature for us to draw on. It just doesn't exist. Even the existing literature doesn't really suit our needs for concerts and recordings. No one had ever even done much transcription for brass quintet before we started. We've had to commission a composer or arranger for every piece we've done. That takes a great deal of planning and development. A string quartet or symphony orchestra can just buy or rent music that they've programmed and be done with it. We can't do that. It's a disadvantage that has become an advantage, because since it's been a necessity to create literature for ourselves, then we've been able to tailor our repertory to our tastes and needs. It also means that we also invest much more money into our programming than most ensembles, because those commissions and custom arrangements don't come cheap! The thing is, we can only wind up performing about 10% of what we buy from composers and arrangers. The other 90% just doesn't work for us in a satisfying way before an audience, even though we might really like the music.

Do you use different programming in different countries where you're performing?

Gene: That sounds so logical when you say it. But what we've discovered is that if something works well in one place, it will probably work well everywhere else. If a piece works for the audience in Toronto, it will probably work in Munich and Tokyo and New York. The trickiest thing is to not only select the right pieces for the concert, but to perform them in the most advantageous order, embellished with all our spoken material and introductions. We do lots of shorter pieces on our concerts. If the applause becomes less and less after each piece, then you're definitely doing something wrong. It should build with each piece as the evening progresses. It's very interesting to hear applause from 150 different audiences in the space of a year. You become a very good judge of not only the volume and enthusiasm of the applause, but also the feeling behind it. Encores become particularly important, because you want to end with the most possible momentum.

You've recorded more than two dozen albums now. Does it become more difficult to come up with album concepts?

Gene: Well… yes and no. That sounds like my standard answer, doesn't it? Presently we have several recording projects in development and consideration. In one respect I think it really depends on the support and cooperation you have with the A & R *(artist and repertoire)* people at your recording label. The people we're working with at Philips now are very supportive, and in that kind of environment it's much easier to come up with album

above:
With Ren
Schilke.

In rehearsal.

concepts because you know they'll take them seriously, and that they have your best interests in mind as well as their own. On the other hand, you do feel the need to create new material that will be as strong a statement as your best work of the past. The growth has to continue. For a performing career to build, the higher it gets, the more energy it takes to grow. Also, it seems that the older you get, the more deliberate and considered your decisions become, which in itself can make settling on projects more difficult.

What do you see in the future for the Canadian Brass?

Gene: Our recording career is really central to what we're doing now, and while it's bad luck to discuss things before they're done, I can just say that we will continue to expand our repertory on recordings in new ways and new styles of music for us. We're getting very involved with trying to have a positive effect on music education in North America, and that's really become our "cause" as a group. There's been so much erosion in the last decade in that area. And of course, we'll continue performing concerts. We're particularly excited about how our career is gaining momentum in Europe. What it really means is that we're building a broader based worldwide audience for the Canadian Brass.

Why do you think that the Canadian Brass has remained successful for so long?

Gene: I don't really have a conclusive explanation for that. It's really the kind of thing that people outside the group would perhaps be able to explain better than me. But I do have ideas, of course, about why we've been successful. We've worked hard in a very directed way. We've always tried to maintain a very positive outlook. We've invested a great deal into developing a very eclectic repertory. And I think that we play well and that we're good performers. But more than anything else, we've offered audiences something that is entirely unique—something that they can't find in any other group. I mean, the whole idea of taking a brass quintet into the kind of performing territory we've thrived in is pretty unique.

What do you feel when you look back on all of this?

Gene: It feels like everything I went through before the Canadian Brass really prepared me for it—the Dixieland roots, the classical study, the orchestral playing, all the contemporary music, the meditation—it all comes into the picture and has been applied to the Canadian Brass. When we play Dixieland, especially, is when I feel like the little Missouri boy's finally back home. When you get to a certain age everybody can look back on their life, and see how things have led to where you are. But I truly feel that about what I've done. Nothing happened suddenly. It was a steady progression of events. And I feel like we've got a long way to go from here, but that we're certainly prepared to tackle whatever comes along. In this business, we're constantly answering the public's unspoken question, "You've gotten our attention. So now what are you going to do?"

CHINESE CAPERS—
MUSIC AND POLITICS

China, 1974. The communist regime had been openly hostile to Western culture for decades. In this year, even in the wake of Nixon's recent diplomatic mission, the Chinese government declared radical and official warfare on all things from the West. Urged by Mme. Chiang, wife to communist leader Mao Tse-Tung, a campaign began which militantly insisted on revolutionary party themes in all art. Western "decadent bourgeois music" was no exception. Rarely heard in previous decades, for three years the music of not only Elvis and the Beatles, but of Bach and Beethoven was not simply discouraged—it was officially banned in China.

By 1977, after three years of unprecedented artistic persecution, the government's radical agenda began to crumble. The death of Mao in 1976 had been a severe blow to Mme. Chiang's power, and party propaganda against Western culture noticeably softened. It was at this crucial time in twentieth century political history that it became clear to diplomatic observers that, for economic and political reasons, China was ever so cautiously flirting with the West. At a time when China and the U.S. were still unable to advance even to a symbolic understanding, Canadian Prime Minister Pierre Trudeau was at the forefront of the diplomatic progress. Early in 1977, in this political atmosphere of tension and hope, it was announced that China and Canada would engage in a milestone cultural exchange. The Shanghai Ballet would tour Canada. Who would Trudeau send in response to represent his country?

The Canadian government needed to choose an artistically world-class ensemble of some kind, one that would communicate good will in the friendliest manner, and whose art would bridge the obvious language barrier with Chinese audiences. As is usually the case in politics, money played somewhat of a role in the

decision. On such short notice the Department of External Affairs could appropriate an emergency budget of only $25,000 for the venture. That, along with logistical reasons, elimated the other serious candidate, the Toronto Symphony. The obvious front-runner choice for this diplomatic trip became those five wild and crazy guys from Toronto, The Canadian Brass.

In March 1977 the Canadian Brass made a remarkable fourteen-day, fourteen-city tour of China, along with their manager, David Haber, Canadian cultural attaché Graeme McDonald, and a journalist from the Toronto paper *The Globe and Mail*. (No American journalist was allowed into the country at the time.) It was a once in a lifetime opportunity. Perhaps never again in history will there be such a prominent culture so systematically segregated from the outside world. And as a result, perhaps there will never be the opportunity for such a radically "alien" musical tour as the Canadian Brass was afforded. As one member of the group has stated, "In a way, it was like visiting another planet. To us in the West at that time, China was this mysteriously secluded, exotic home to a billion people. We were just as exotic to them. We would have been celebrities there even if we'd never played a note, because just the way we looked and the language we spoke was to them a rare curiosity. They just liked staring at us."

(A full and colorful report of the Chinese adventure appears later in this chapter,written collectively by the members of the quintet, and published in a magazine article in 1977.)

The tour was a resounding success. Everywhere the Brass went, they were treated with hospitality, warmth and high regard, like visiting royalty. *The Beijing People's Daily* hailed the tour as a clear signal of the dawn of a new China, and "pays tribute to the Canadian quintet for presenting to the Chinese audience a program that is varied in forms and styles. Their excellent skill, fidelity in interpretation and lively, bright and vivacious performance have left the audience with a deep impression."

Suddenly these five not particularly political musicians were thrust into a political context that gave them international headlines across Europe and North America. It was a publicist's dream come true. No amount of concerts or television appearances or recordings could ever attain anything like the worldwide coverage the Canadian Brass received from the Chinese tour. "Chinese praise Canadian Brass" headlined *The Toronto Star*. *The Daily Telegraph* in London reported that "China has welcomed in unusually warm terms a series of concerts by the Canadian Brass." It was the same story all over the western world—almost. Curiously enough, unbeknownst to the players, the one journalist actually touring with the Brass, Ross Munro of *The Globe and Mail* (who was also by de facto covering the tour for American papers), was sending back steadily negative reports of the tour, headlines like "Polite Chinese find Brass too far out," and "The Canadian Brass blows hot and cold for the People's Republic." His reports were often along these lines: "Their hotel [in Changsha] is a real comedown... The rooms are dirty... The food turns out to be awful... The Brass is in awful shape for the concert. They butcher Bach." When the quintet returned to Toronto and read Munro's reports they were furious. Chuck explains:

> First of all, he was a political animal on a musical tour. He was totally insensitive to their protocol in concerts and how that affected their responses as audiences. He embarrassed us constantly throughout the trip. We would go and meet with the Chinese artists after they performed for us, and they'd say, 'Well, is there anything you'd like to ask us?' We'd inquire about what they had performed for us, about their training, about their disciplines and their art, which is fascinating and very different from our traditions. In general, it was usually a conversation between performing artists who were curious about one another's art and lives. Time and again Ross would interrupt the friendly, easy flow of things with pointed political questions. It was embarrassing for us and for the Chinese. They weren't at all accustomed to discussing politics publicly. Besides, the whole point of our being there was a friendly cultural exchange, with a political objective to be sure, but not with a political agenda. It was like he was trying to be some kind of major league foreign correspondent stirring up whatever political controversy he could. It wasn't an appropriate way to cover the tour. He wasn't adept at truly covering the subtle and fascinating political observations that one couldn't help but make on such a cultural exchange, so he tried to muscle up what I'm sure he thought was more pointedly political substance. And, oh yeah—be a music critic at the same time.

Fortunately, there were foreign journalists giving a more balanced report elsewhere. Despite Ross Munro, the tour was one of the two major turning points in the Brass' long career (the other being the record contract with RCA).

An account of what it was like to tour China just as the Reign of Terror was ending, and the Brass' reaction to Munro's reporting, is best expressed in an article published in a 1977 issue of the Canadian magazine *Performing Arts*, written collectively by all five members, and presented here with few cuts. This description is of a culture that has changed rapidly and drastically since that time, though certainly still struggling with its political objectives and its relationship with the West. Some things encountered today by the many Western tourists would be vastly different from the Canadian Brass' encounters. After all, they were literally some of the first Westerners allowed on an extensive tour of the country in twenty years or so—a privilege not granted to heads of state or ambassadors, but to a gentle band of musicians. In 1977, touring China with a brass quintet was about as far as a musician or anyone else could personally go in pushing the envelope for worldliness, and to have been there as pioneering, peaceful ambassadors, in wide-eyed discovery of a hidden, bustling, ancient culture in the midst of major social change, must have been thoroughly amazing...

"Everything went off the way it was supposed to and the Chinese couldn't have been warmer or friendlier. When we arrived at the Beijing airport on the evening of March 10th, we were received by about a dozen people. It was just like in the newsreels. There was this gigantic picture of Chairman Mao, in beautiful colour. The effect was staggering...They ushered us into a special waiting room where we were given tea and messages of welcome. From then on, we had no further worries about passports, baggage or anything. Everything was done for us.

"The next day, after a morning visit to the Imperial Palace and the Chinese Friendship Committee's welcoming luncheon, we gave our first performance, actually a rehearsal for the official evening concert. We had a full house both times, with the audiences supposedly made up of an invited cross-section of society—workers, peasants, soldiers, officials, students, and people in the arts. Actually, it was hard to tell because they all

top: Canton Friendship Hall
middle: Tea and speeches at the Beijing airport
bottom: Impromptu concert at Shaoshan, birthplace of Mao

dressed pretty much the same. At the luncheon banquet, one Chinese official had told us, 'The Chinese may have a look of stone on their faces, but don't be put off by that; they're really very warm. As time goes on, you'll feel the friendship.' This was very true. We didn't see much expression, except sometimes a little twinkle in the eye here and there, but all through China they stressed the whole idea of friendship. They seemed convinced that Norman Bethune [a Canadian doctor, famous in China for having made the "Long March" with Mao] had already established a relationship between our two countries. We heard that everywhere.

"For the first evening concert in Beijing, there were many dignitaries, and the reaction was pretty much what we expected. We played and they applauded. There was no thunderous applause, except after 'Song of Liberation,' a Chinese piece. Back in January, when we were first told we were going for sure, we were asked to submit three different programmes, along with scores, recordings and biographies of the composers. Several selections were sent back unapproved—all the ragtime music, plus Canadian contemporary works by John Beckwith, Syd Hodkinson, John Weinzweig and Eldon Rathburn. Everything else was accepted, including contemporary pieces by Harry Freedman, Malcolm Arnold and Karel Husa. That narrowed it down to two programmes, and when we arrived in Beijiing we were told they had also decided to eliminate the Husa. Instead, they gave us three Chinese pieces to look at. They didn't ask us to perform them, but we decided to substitute them for the Husa.

"So that first day we played Renaissance pieces by Pezel, Malcolm Arnold's Quintet, Malcolm Forsyth's 'Golyardes' Grounde,' the Chinese 'Song of Liberation,' Freedman's "Five Rings"—a work written for the Olympics, but the Chinese said it would be better if the Olympics weren't mentioned—Purcell's 'Trumpet Sonata,' Bach's 'Little Fugue in G Minor,' and the 'Toccata and Fugue in D Minor,' Howard Cable's arrangement of the Chinese song, 'Sailing the Sea Depends on the Helmsman,' and for an encore, Larry Crossley's 'Days Before Yesterday,' a comedy piece where we run around chairs.

top: The Red Army Band joins the Brass
bottom: Chairman Mao oversees concert at a Canton middle
school.

"Now, we had been warned by the Chinese not to get upset because audiences in China don't respond the same as audiences in the West. They applaud and they're very polite, but that's all. And they seemed very self-conscious, too. First, a row of dignitaries comes in and the audience stands up to applaud their leaders. Then the people would watch very closely to see how to respond to our concert. They wouldn't applaud until they saw the leaders applauding, and even though we would have liked to get the audience to really let loose, they wouldn't because the leaders didn't. So that explains the 'polite' reaction we got. It's also significant that Munro wrote that 'the music was far too modern or obscure' for the Canadian diplomats, too. That's bound to happen when you play any serious music for a group of diplomats—they're going to freak out because they don't know anything about music! No one ever told us, though, not to play any of our pieces, and despite Munro's claim that we scrapped most of our prepared pieces, we only dropped two, the Arnold and the Freedman. That's the kind of thing we do anywhere, adjusting our programmes to get the best general response...

"Of course, we couldn't talk to our audiences the way we do at home, but we did manage to communicate a bit by mime. At Chinese concerts, an announcer calls out the name of each piece and composer before it is played, and for the Gabrieli, we prepared a sight gag. First, four of us walked down from the stage and went to all four corners of the auditorium. That impressed them to begin with. Then we had Chuck come out on stage and start looking for us while the announcer said in Chinese, 'The tuba begins this piece.' At that, Chuck would point to himself and mime the words, 'Wa?— me?' in Chinese, and everyone would break up.

"We wound up playing 14 concerts in 14 days, and everywhere we went people knew who we were. In Guangzhow, we arrived at the concert hall and thought there was a football game or something going on, there were so many people. All the tickets had already been given out—they weren't sold—and so many people had wanted to see us that there was almost a riot when they couldn't get in... We couldn't overlook the political significance of our concerts. We were told that the Bach we performed was the first Bach to be heard in China since the Cultural Revolution, and the Chinese were making this an obvious fact by taping our first concert and then broadcasting four different 20-minute programmes all over China, and even all over the world via shortwave.

"Of course, we knew that in China, going along with what Mao said, there was no such thing as art for art's sake. The music we were playing was exemplary of a political message, that of Chinese friendship with Canada and their new willingness to expose their people to Western music. The whole tour had been set up for this purpose, and the publicity coverage was incredible. Photographers and interviewers from Radio Beijing followed us everywhere, even when we played on top of the Great Wall and in the gardens of the Ming Tombs... We always took our instruments with us, to show our willingness to play wherever we went, and when we arrived at Mao's shrine, in his home town of Shaoshan, we found they had arranged for us to play, if we wanted to, an impromptu outdoor concert near the farmhouse where Mao was born. So we said sure, and after having lunch and seeing the shrine, we started to play. In a matter of minutes we had audience of at least 600 people. Since the work week is staggered—one seventh of the population gets one day off on a different day of the week—there were always swarms of people around the museums and shrines. They had pre-planned this concert, of course, but they laid it on us very gradually and didn't make us feel we *had* to play. The same thing happened after our sightseeing tour of a porcelain factory in Changsha. We finished the tour in the shipping area and *there* were our instruments, which we had left in the little van we travelled in. A little stage had been set up, too. That's when we knew we were going to play a concert! But it was terrific—we felt we got a much more honest response from these audiences. There was an openness and a much freer relationship without having officials around, and we got incredible reactions.

"We gave one performance for the army band in Beijing, and they played for us, too. They were easily as good as the Canadian Armed Forces Band, but they were all very humble when they spoke to us—'We feel we've learned so much seeing you

112

perform,' they said. One of them went up to Ronnie, a fellow trumpet player, and patted himself on the chest and then patted Ronnie on the chest. It was his beautiful way of communicating that he really loved what was going on.

"From Beijing we went to Wuhan, a steel manufacturing town that was very active in terms of the arts. We saw a ballet class and a rehearsal of an opera. A tenor soloist sang, and some women did folk dances. The opera orchestra used both native and Western instruments and made a really unusual sound. Then we played for all of them... A troupe of kids called the Little Red Guards put on a whole evening's entertainment for us, singing, dancing, and playing instruments. The oldest were about 15, the youngest about 7, but they were all highly skilled, polished and assured. Even the very youngest ones had a great deal of presence, and they seemed to be having fun, too... We were intrigued to find out how they stream kids in the educational system, how they find talent and how talented kids are treated differently, getting specialized schooling and better living quarters. In Guangzhow, we also visited a regular middle school. It was very heartening; the kids were like any other junior high school kids. We were shocked, though, by the English lesson—'Is he a good boy?' 'Yes, he follows the teachings of the Party.'

"One thing that is really different in China is the role of music and musicians. Every city has its song and dance troupe or an opera company, but these groups are really propaganda teams. That's why they may be treated a little better—they have to go out and convince the peasants how bad it was before the Revolution. We asked how performers managed to keep up their training if everyone is supposed to pitch in sometime to work on the land in a commune. We were told that a dance or musical group would go to the fields and live on the commune but that they would perform for the peasants and not have to go out and do the crops themselves.

"A scary aspect of the arts in China was made plain to us at one of our banquets. Chuck was seated next to a Chinese trombone player and asked to be introduced to a fellow tuba player. The trombone player looked embarrassed and answered through an

above: A vintage communist shot—on a makeshift stage, playing for workers in a porcelain factory.
below: Enjoying a group of children performing

interpreter, 'Well, he's out doing some other work now.' It seems that a few years ago, when Chiang Ching, Mao's wife, was in charge of culture, she went to a concert of the Beijing Philharmonic and decided she didn't like the sound the tuba made. So she had the guy fired, and that became an example for the whole country—all the tuba players in all the orchestras were fired. So now there are no tubas in the orchestras!*... All the arts carry a political message. We saw ballets, operas and the famous film 'The East Is Red.' All of them tell the same basic story, in which the people, usually led by a very strong, very masculine woman, destroy their oppressors—landlords or foreigners. There's never any love interest. They seldom touch each other, even in the ballet. People aren't lovers, they're comrades. After we watched one show where the landlords were getting hacked up, Fred turned to the interpreter and told him that he was a landlord himself since he rented part of his ten-room house to tenants; that all five of us were capitalists, since we worked for ourselves, and that we paid David Haber to take care of our management. The interpreter had assumed that David was our leader and told us what to do. He was dumbfounded by all this...

"Still, we noticed that there was no discussion of political or social things unless we brought them up. None of the Chinese asked us any questions and seemed reluctant to answer any questions about politics, too. But Ross Munro's interests were primarily political, not artistic. We had a press conference in Wuhan where Ross started throwing all kinds of political questions, trying to pin them against the wall. This got worse as the tour went on and we all started getting a bit nervous. The Chinese Friendship Committee told David Haber that they were upset and that this was not what our tour was all about. David's reaction was to ask whether Ross had to be on the tour at all, and if he stayed, whether he could keep his mouth shut and just write about what we were there to do. Ross got wind of this and said to us, 'One thing I'm not going to be is a PR agent for you. This has nothing to do with you guys, but that David Haber—I'm going to get him!' From then on, things got worse and worse, and Ross kept

*Later the Brass found out that it was actually a bass trombonist she had disliked, but the conductor had blamed the tuba player!

making more of an ass of himself. Even though he told us that he would put all kinds of glowing things in his final article, we got quite a shock when we actually saw it.

"In Changsha, *he* didn't like the meal and he blamed it on us. We had been getting meal after meal in fantastic gourmet style, but in Changsha the food wasn't as good as it had been. So what? Sometimes in northern Ontario, you can't find *anything* good to eat. It's true, as he wrote, that the butter was rancid, but that was because we requested butter and probably the last time anyone had requested butter was eight years ago, and this was the same butter! Munro also criticized the hotel, but again those were *his* feelings, not ours. He should have looked around at the houses in the town—no electricity, no running water, everyone was living in shacks, and in comparison we were living like kings. If he thought that hotel was bad, he should see some of the hotels we've stayed at in Canada! We had no reason to complain. Wherever we went, they gave us the very best they could and bent over backwards to please us, even to finding some butter no one had used for ages.

"Ross remained uptight, though, and described the audience in Changsha as giving us 'barely polite applause' when they weren't being 'openly restless.' But we noticed whenever we went to an opera or ballet that this is the way Chinese audiences are—there will be a lot of conversation during the performance and hardly any applause after, even though *we* applauded like crazy. We also had to remember that we were playing for people who had never heard a brass quintet before and whose musical experience was terribly limited—the only repertoire they knew was the official party music, the same 20 or so ballet and opera tunes that are played over and over and over again. We still had the feeling that every time we played they felt really lucky to be able to hear us... Every place we went, we were met at the door. If it was cold, they gave us hot washcloths. If it was warm, they gave us cold washcloths. Then we'd sit down and have tea...

"We asked to see an instrument factory, and like dummies we assumed we'd see them making brass instruments. But they took us to a violin factory; the brass factory was too far away. So we

saw violins being made and then sat down for tea, and all of a sudden a bunch of guys walked in with brass instruments under their arms—they had brought the brass factory people to us!

"Wherever we went, and we were allowed to go anywhere we wanted, we found friendliness and curiosity. When we walked through streets or went into stores, crowds followed us and kids point at us, yelling 'Foreigners!' in Chinese to each other. We were allowed to take pictures of everything except the 2,000-year-old woman. The Friendship Committee assigned people to serve as guides and interpreters, but we were free to split up and walk around any time we wanted, even without any Chinese along. The only thing they were afraid of was that we might get lost and not be able to ask our way back. We dressed casually, even for concerts and banquets. We had been told 'no tails,' and at one point, when we wondered if we should wear suits for a banquet, our interpreter said that in China, people aren't concerned about what you wear and it was more important that we were comfortable. So we went in the clothes we usually wore—turtlenecks and jeans— and we *were* comfortable. We were impressed that the Chinese people we met *also* seemed comfortable and involved in whatever they were doing. They seemed to have a genuine sense of participation in building a new China.

"When the time came to part, the Chinese people who had been with us on the tour started crying—it was so emotional. We exchanged gifts. They had completely documented our tour and gave us each a beautiful photo album with a complete set of pictures. We gave them Eskimo prints and some records..."

It seems improbable that an entourage from Canada, who were certainly accustomed to cold weather, would not take adequate winter clothing for a March tour of China. They were loaned the standard issue, military-looking Chinese winter coats for the tour. In addition, they all went out right away and bought what they called "Mao hats" to complete the ensemble. It's that fashionable

above: Chuck with an embalmed, resurrected Mao-Tse-Tung—Not. He's actually the president of the Friendship Association.

below: Gene with a filthy capitalist inquiry, "Can you make me this plate? You could export them and we'd all get rich."

revolutionary look in the photos that makes it seem as if they're engaged in some fierce cultural identification, at least to us. To one Chinese woman, the sight of an unexpected, alien-looking man, (taller than your average comrade) clad in an imposing, oversized coat and hat was just too much.

One day in Beijing the guys had gone to what was basically a department store to buy the aforementioned "Mao hats." As Chuck and Ron were walking down a flight of stairs, a petite Chinese lady started up the stairs, head and eyes down. As Ron got nearer to her, she first saw his boots. And reminiscent of a hundred Hollywood scenes, she slowly panned her vision up his, from her perspective, monster tall body, perched a few steps above her, wearing what she must have thought was the biggest coat ever made. Her eyes hesitantly landed on sweet Ron's fully bearded face, framed by a pretty serious looking, huge hat with fur trim and king-sized earflaps. By now the little Chinese woman was off-balance and gasping in horror—after all, there had been a "Reign of Terror" for ten years. As Ron reached and grabbed her, steadying her from falling backwards, she began wailing and wailing, apparently convinced that some kind of Party monster had come for her at last.

CHASING RAINBOWS—
RECORDING

There is a basic truth that has become a gospel of 20th century musical life: to have any kind of noteworthy career you must regularly make recordings, released on a major label. Whether you're Enrico Caruso, the Beatles, Madonna, or the Canadian Brass, it's your recordings that will make or break an international career. Even with a group as committed to performing live concerts as the Brass, the fact is that you can only play for just so many people in just so many places in any given season. And in the case of the Brass' recording career, they owe it all to Queen Elizabeth. More on that later. Let's backtrack a bit first...

It's not every musical ensemble that can claim that its first major performance was recorded and broadcast nationally over radio. But since the Canadian Brass is the Canadian Brass, that's just the way their recording career began. Gene had many contacts at CBC from the broadcasts he had played as a member of the Toronto Symphony. From the quintet's outset, they had interested parties at CBC who basically said, "Go get your act together, and when you're ready, we'll make a radio show." After about a year of rehearsal the Brass must have indeed been ready, because in 1971 the CBC recorded what was the ensemble's first major performance in Toronto. This wasn't simply a run-of-the-mill recorded live concert broadcast that one might normally hear on the public radio. The material from the 1971 concert was combined with recorded material from a 1972 appearance and an actual record resulted. It was a beginning.*

The Canadian Brass would return to the recording studio relatively quickly with an album project done with the Festival

*Material from these recordings was re-released under the title "The Canadian Brass—Encore" on the Musica Viva label, part of CBC Enterprises, in Canada in 1987, and at this writing is still available for sale.

In the studio, late 1977, recording in the Direct-to-Disk format.

Singers of Canada, conducted by Elmer Iseler. This album of music for choir and brass, entitled "Make We Joy," was recorded following the Brass' European tour with the chorus, along with several concert broadcasts with Iseler.*

Getting back to Queen Elizabeth...if we discount the first ventures onto vinyl cited above, The Canadian Brass can thank HRH for truly launching their commercial recording career. It came about like this: One day in 1973 the quintet was invited to play at the new Shaw Theatre on Niagara-on-the-Lake, Ontario. Their job was to play music that greeted the guest of honor for the occasion, none other than Queen Elizabeth. The scheduled time for the queen's arrival came and went, but since the queen is never late, of course, (protocol dictates that everyone else is early instead) the Brass simply kept playing to entertain the assembled, anxious crowd. The royal entourage hadn't yet showed, but during the delay the Canadian Brass virtually played an entire concert that had been completely unplanned. HRH finally arrived, and the official ceremony went on as planned. Eleanor Snyderman, then wife of Canadian record mogul "Sam, the Record Man" Snyderman, heard their performance that day, and was more than impressed with how the Brass so easily covered a very tense situation in a very entertaining manner. Eleanor had been contemplating a record label that would venture into the classical/crossover market. It couldn't have been a better time for Canadian Brass. She decided that these guys were just special enough to take a chance on, and signed the Brass for the first projects in the Boot Master Concert Series.

The first Boot Records project was recorded in 1973, entitled simply "Canadian Brass." It's a very nice record, but the sessions for that first album pale in the quintet's memory compared to the quintet's next album. Entitled "Canadian Brass in Paris," this was recorded in the acoustically perfect but impractical locale of the famous St. Chapelle Cathedral. The crew had to rent a mobile recording unit, and everyone arrived at the site only to find that somehow the arrangements had not quite been communicated to the guards there. Only after a cash bribe was the troupe allowed

*It's interesting to note that the Brass has continued recording with this choral group as recently as 1990.

into the sanctuary. All the recording had to be done at night when the historic chapel was closed to visitors. The resulting album was an artistic success, but a financial nightmare. Costs of recording on location in Paris were so high that even though sales were strong, the accountants saw red on that project for several years.

One of the Brass' last Canadian record ventures, in 1976, was a CBC-backed release entitled "Unexplored Territory," and is unusual among their recordings. This was very much a studio project, involving multi-tracking and Don Gillis' arrangements featuring the Brass with Don's jazz quartet. The quintet's final project on a strictly Canadian label was a 1977 direct-to-disk album, simply entitled "The Canadian Brass," an Umbrella release. This was a recording process that predated digital technology, and was only used for a brief time in the industry. It required the performers to record an entire side of an album in one sitting, from start to finish, with only a few seconds break between numbers. The process avoided tape entirely, and the master for duplication was an actual record disk. As anyone can imagine, it made for a slightly more stressful session than usual. The Brass loved the challenge. Because of the strict demands on the performers, where it was well-known that no editing was possible, the project also was clear evidence to the world of what the Canadian Brass was capable of in live performance.

By 1977 the quintet was being managed in New York by Kazuko Hillyer, who was trying to introduce the group to the executives at RCA. By coincidence, the RCA marketing manager, Irwin Katz, heard the Brass on one of New York's classical stations, WQXR. The station had a program on Friday mornings called "The Listening Room" with host Bob Sherman, and the Canadian Brass were the live, profiled guests on the day when Mr. Katz happened to be listening. By the time their manager had arranged a meeting for the Brass with Thomas Z. Shepard, vice president of RCA Red Seal, Mr. Katz had already told him about this wonderful brass group he had heard on the radio. It's all part of the kind of luck that has graced the Canadian Brass throughout the years.

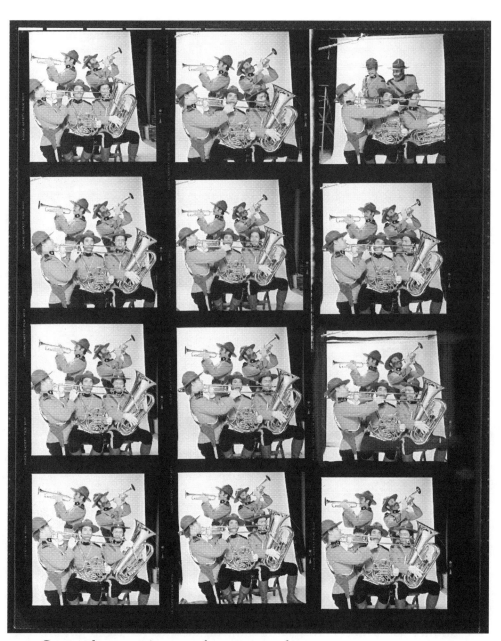

Cover photo session proofs, never used.

Gene tells the story of that first meeting with Shepard:

> The meeting was set up by our manager, Kazuko Hillyer. We spent about an hour talking about doing recordings, and whether we would be on the label or not. He had heard that we were very creative and interesting guys, and we were kind of nervous and weren't being either creative or interesting. It didn't feel like it was going well. As we were walking out the door he said, 'By the way, do you guys have any Fats Waller?' We looked at one another and said, with great enthusiasm, 'Oh yeah! We love Fats Waller.' I'm not sure, but I don't think we had played any Fats Waller up to that moment, but we weren't going to tell him that. We were more than happy to learn whatever Tom Shepard wanted to hear. He said, 'Well, I'm just now recording *Ain't Misbehavin,*' which is hot right now. Maybe if you guys could come up with some Fats Waller material, we could do an album of that.' It all came together very quickly after that. At the time we were playing at the Beacon Theatre on Broadway, and quickly had come up with some Waller arrangements and put them into our program. Jay Saks, producer at RCA, heard our show and liked the arrangments. And within about a week we were in the studio doing our first album for RCA. That's the first time we met Luther Henderson. We didn't have enough Waller material to fill out an album, so Tom Shepard contacted Luther Henderson about doing some arrangements for us. Luther had just done arranging and orchestrating for *Ain't Misbehavin'* on Broadway, so he was a natural choice. What an important day that turned out to be. Luther has been our principal arranger for non-classical material since that day. It's amazing, but he had never before written for brass quintet until he wrote those Waller arrangements for us. We played through them and immediately recognized a master.

The album, recorded in 1978, was originally released under the title "Mostly Fats," and has since been retitled "Ain't Misbehavin'". (No reason has been stated for the title change, but maybe RCA came to believe that "Mostly Fats" made it sound like an album by a majority of overeaters.) As the original title indicates, the contents of the album are not entirely confined to music by Fats Waller. Not only had the Brass landed a contract with one of the world's major record labels, they had also begun working with a major league producer in Jay Saks, a Grammy-winning record producer who had regularly worked with the Chicago Symphony and the Philadelphia Orchestra, and they had formed a relationship with master arranger Luther Henderson. In 1977 the quintet had grabbed international headlines for their China tour, and now one year later was making albums that would be sold all over the world. It was more than a turning point for them. The next few years, between 1977 and 1979, were when the Canadian Brass went from being a modestly successful Canadian musical ensemble to being an internationally recognized musical attraction.

RCA had some experience with at least one "crossover" artist prior to signing the Canadian Brass. They had been very successful with James Galway, and understood the delicate balance in classical and popular material that is necessary for a crossover career. Between 1978 and 1982 the Brass recorded five albums for RCA: "Ain't Misbehavin'," "Pachelbel Canon and Other Great Baroque Hits," "The Village Band, " "Christmas with the Canadian Brass," and "High, Bright, Light and Clear." The group had a good working relationship with RCA, their albums were hitting the Billboard charts, and sales were excellent. As part of all of this success, their concert career jumped to a new echelon, and they were playing performances in all the major American cities. So if things were so good, then why did the Brass leave RCA to sign with CBS in 1982? In retrospect it's a question that they often asked themselves.

By this time the Brass had toured Japan, and had discovered that they did not have strong record distribution there through RCA. They began to feel that their recordings were not being well-promoted in any international market, nor in the States and Canada. One record was particularly late in coming out, and that upset them a bit. The fact that they were getting more attention than anyone might have ever expected for a brass quintet didn't enter into their thoughts at the time. The contract came due for renegotiating, and CBS made it known that it was interested in the Brass. Other pastures always seem greener.

This was 1982, and CBS had just been hailed as the top crossover label of the year, on the basis of an album recorded by Placido Domingo with John Denver. Gene explains the situation:

top: Fred with RCA producer Jay Saks.
bottom: A toast to the completed album, "Brass in Berlin," with the Berlin Philharmonic players, and another Grammy-winning producer, James Mallinson (bottom right), 1983.

We were sitting there thinking, 'Well, we've done great with RCA. We like the people there, the marketing staff, and our producer. We like Tom.' It seems RCA thought everything was fine and they were confident about resigning us. Our lawyer felt that he was not getting a response from RCA when it was time to negotiate. Unfortunately, we didn't know the current sales figures for our RCA albums were booming at the time. There was definitely some miscommunication. By the time we had sorted it all out, we were past the point of no return in negotiating a contract with CBS. Somehow we were persuaded that CBS was more expert in the crossover market, and also that they promised simultaneous release for us of any new album into all international markets. It was even in our contract. The truth is that in the end we felt bad about leaving RCA, because personally we liked them so much. Almost immediately after we signed with CBS we began to see the value of the friendly relationship we had had at RCA, because our dealings were difficult with CBS from the beginning and remained that way throughout our contract there. The whole idea that CBS was expert in the crossover market was a complete snow job. They didn't seem to know or care a thing about it. We had to A & R our own projects from the start, with little guidance or support from them.

"A & R" (artist and repertoire) is a recording industry term referring to the work with recording artists in choosing and developing appropriate and opportune projects. This could mean interpreting market research and sales to give artists guidance into what kind of concepts would be the best career moves to which the record-buying public might be most receptive. It can also mean selecting music, arrangers, producers, and generally being supportive in any way that will ensure that the best possible albums be made. The Canadian Brass maintains that CBS did virtually none of this during their years on the label. The situation was basically, "You've got a contract for two albums a year. Come up with something we'll like. End of input."

The first album at CBS was an experiment for the Brass in a new musical direction, recording pop style arrangements with keyboards and drums of several rock tunes. Entitled "Champions," the album was an odd first outing for the quintet at CBS, and there are mixed reactions about the results. Some have observed that perhaps the arrangements simply weren't strong enough. Others seemed to like hearing the ensemble in a more casual, laid back musical outing. Whatever the musical results, CBS didn't seem to understand the album and how to market it, nor, according to Chuck Daellenbach, did the record label make any serious attempt to get the album into record stores.

The next CBS project, in 1983, was an interesting project entitled "Brass in Berlin," a double quintet album recorded in Germany with players from the Berlin Philharmonic. In a rare move that was advantageous to the Brass, CBS assigned them a world-class producer, James Mallinson. Chuck speaks:

> We had a wonderful, very positive experience working on the Berlin album with Mallinson. He was excited about working with us, and we began to discuss with him ideas for future projects. We telexed to CBS that the album was going great, and that we were excited about a terrific concept for the next album, a recording of the complete 'Art of the Fugue' by Bach, which was a project we had very much wanted to do since the inception of the Canadian Brass. The response was very frosty. Something like, 'It is not the duty of the producer to be doing A&R work on new projects, and that this was a subject to be addressed upon our return to New York.' That set the hostile tone for the rest of the days at CBS.

With "Art of the Fugue" languishing with CBS' disinterest, along with 10 or 12 recording concepts presented by the Brass that CBS dismissed without serious consideration, the quintet hit upon the idea of a "live" album. CBS resisted, but eventually gave reluctant approval so that the Brass could fulfill their obligation to record 3 albums in a two year period. One cut on the record is "Boy Mozart," a rock novelty number that features the players singing witty lyrics about Wolfgang as a superstar prodigy. The song required some multitracking and remixing in the studio, which CBS was unwilling to pay for. Chuck:

> The song needed studio work to bring it up to standards, and even though CBS refused to fund the work required, we decided we had no choice but to pay for it ourselves. That was a recurring theme with our recordings with that label. We always wound up paying for recording costs because they simply refused to give us the money we needed to make the albums meet reasonable professional standards.

The Brass' enthusiasm for recording "The Art of the Fugue" hadn't died, and they somehow had received approval to proceed with the project with the helpful influence of a newfound ally in the

Cover photo for the "Live" album, 1985.

CBS marketing division. Rehearsals were in full swing, and all the arrangements for the recording dates had been made. Then two weeks before the scheduled recording, the A & R representative stated, "We've decided that we don't want you to record 'The Art of the Fugue' unless you can come up with a famous composer to finish the piece." (Bach's most complex masterwork was left unfinished at his death, although the piece is very performable, as all the musical world knows.) The Brass was stunned at what seemed a ridiculous directive, and who could blame them? Even if they could find a reputable composer who would risk the thankless venture, finishing "The Art of the Fugue," quite possibly the single most profound musical accomplishment in Baroque music, would be like some present day painter finishing the Sistine Chapel. Why would anyone pretend to be on equal footing with the legendary musical god J. S. Bach? CBS was either revealing highly questionable musical judgment, or was playing a game to avoid the project. However incredulous, the Brass collected themselves to respond, "O.K., if you say so. We've got the Vivaldi 'Four Seasons' ready to record. Let's go with that." A & R was unsupportive of the idea, but it turned out that the head of the label, Joe Dash, was very enthusiastic about the Vivaldi piece, so the project was reluctantly approved. With only two weeks to rehearse and prepare "The Art of the Fugue" became "The Four Seasons," which was the Canadian Brass' fourth album at CBS. Listening to the exciting, virtuoso performances on that recording, it's difficult to believe that the project was put together so quickly. (Arthur Frackenpohl's transcriptions for The Canadian Brass of "The Art of the Fugue" and "The Four Seasons" are certainly landmarks in the brass quintet repertoire.)

Another Christmas album, a sequel to the earlier RCA release, came next, and continued the Brass' relationship with arranger Luther Henderson. As with the earlier holiday album, it turned out to be a perennial bestseller. But true to form, the project was not without the by now expected CBS discord. A & R informed the Brass that "Go Tell It on the Mountain" was not a Christmas title, and therefore was inappropriate material for the album. (The lyrics to the chorus of this world famous spiritual are "Go tell it on the mountain/Over the hills and everywhere/Go tell it on the

Luther Henderson, principal arranger for the Brass, has worked on hundreds of projects over the decades, including arranging on Broadway with Richard Rodgers, adapting the music for *Ain't Misbehavin'*, and the musical conception and musical realization for *Jelly's Last Jam*.

mountain/That Jesus Christ is born.") And since that deleted title would make the record too short, then the recording schedule would need to be delayed until the title could be replaced. They further argued that the result of all this would mean that the release of the album would be delayed another year. The Brass decided that it would be more persuasive to let the arranger, Luther Henderson, respond. His succinct, diplomatic response was: "Well, I guess it all depends on which church you go to." It apparently cast some doubts at CBS about their position. "Go Tell It on the Mountain" was approved, the recording proceeded as scheduled, and the album, "A Canadian Brass Christmas" was an immediate bestseller.

Dixieland is a style that has appealed to the Canadian Brass, and doing an album of this music seemed like a natural idea. While touring in Los Angeles the Brass met the head of west coast marketing for CBS, Roger Holdridge, who was a big Dixieland fan and a strong supporter of the Brass. He saw them as the true crossover group, one that appeals to classical fans as well as to people who have grown up listening to rock and pop music but are ready to move on to broaden their musical tastes. Holdridge moved to CBS headquarters in New York, and although he wasn't in the A & R department, he worked with the Brass in choosing material for the album that would be released under the title "Basin Street." Once again Luther Henderson was asked to do the arrangements, and once again, it was a masterful job. Henderson had grown up with this music, and had known firsthand some of the musicians who defined and developed the Dixieland style. He looked on this and other collaborations with the Canadian Brass as opportunities to notate in an authentic manner a musical style that is largely lost in the past. His comments (printed on the album cover) reveal an interesting point of view:

> I think it is important to write everything down—in the same fashion that we have the notated variations of Paganini or Liszt. All the great virtuosi performed in a way equivalent to the jazz experience, in that they had some portion of their concert devoted to improvisation. Dixieland is the kind of improvisation that has grown up in America where black-African

above: 1986 recording of "Basin Street" with George Segal in Toronto.
below: George Segal and arranger Luther Henderson.

music traditions were superimposed on imported European marches, church music, and the like. Some of these improvisations became standard, so that we have inherited the riffs, the sounds, the expressions, and a whole musical language called Dixieland—and this can be notated. Mind you, it's very hard to notate anything like that—maybe our writing will become some kind of a new standard. If I can put down on paper whatever I remember from the 30s and 40s, and vicariously from the important earlier twenty years, then I would like to do it. Maybe then we will have captured the essence of Dixieland for all time...for all future performers as well.

"Basin Street" was the first album the Brass recorded with their new horn player, David Ohanian. There was also a rather unlikely guest on the album, the result of a casual chance encounter that Gene had with the actor George Segal. Sitting in a café one day, Gene happened to see Segal walking by. Gene had recently seen him on "The Tonight Show," and George had played banjo with the band. Trailing after him down the sidewalk, Gene introduced himself and the two chatted for awhile. He told George about the Dixieland album, and wondered if he might enjoy playing banjo on a couple of tunes. Segal seemed mildly interested. Phone numbers were exchanged, and by the time Gene returned home late that night there was a series of messages from Segal, each one progressively more insistently excited about the idea. The Brass was excited about the idea too—a Hollywood star guesting on the album certainly wouldn't hurt.

Unfortunately, the contract negotiations between CBS and George Segal for his appearance on the album became snarled. Segal's attitude from the beginning was that this was somewhat of a lark for him, and that he wasn't expecting to make much money at it. He wasn't demanding any royalties. Nevertheless, CBS asked him to sign an exclusive contract agreeing not to record any of the material recorded with the Brass elsewhere for a period of five years. Segal, being an amateur musician, pointed out that he really only played a few tunes, but felt it was unfair to require him to give up any opportunities that might unexpectedly arise (as this one had) for the next five years. CBS then tried to cancel the whole project. On the first scheduled day of recording everyone arrived, including George Segal, along with his unsigned letter of agreement. CBS was unrelenting in its position, but the Brass, supported by producer James Mallinson, were

Cover photo for the "Basin Street" album.

determined. Segal offered to do the job as a side man for scale, which wouldn't require him to sign as an exclusive label artist. The New York executives were still refusing (one wonders why), but the recording proceeded, and George Segal can be heard on four cuts on the finished album. It seemed that the Brass had won the battle, but the war with CBS continued, which leads to an anecdote from Chuck:

> At some point in all our difficulties with CBS there was an exchange of particularly heated correspondence. We were trying to be diplomatic, but it was tough. One letter we wrote back to them ended with the line 'Let's stop this war between us.' Upon re-reading the letter just before it was mailed, I felt that it was a little too strong to call the situation an outright war, but we didn't have time that day to re-do the letter. So I just took a pen and wrote over the letter 'w' in 'war' to make it a 't,' and as a result the last sentence read, 'Let's stop this tar between us.' I know that it didn't make any sense like that, and maybe I was just cutting up a bit. I actually thought they probably wouldn't notice anyway. Maybe it did amuse me to send that little incident of letter graffiti to them.

The situation with CBS took a positive turn when Irwin Katz came into the picture as an executive on the label. A brass player himself, he loved the Canadian Brass and the kind of work they were doing, and had actually been the person to introduce the Brass to RCA a few years earlier. Katz pointed out to his colleagues the excellent sales of the group's albums, far surpassing any of the other artists in the classical/crossover area. He saw how well prepared and rehearsed they came to recording sessions, and how efficiently and inexpensively they could record an album, compared with other ensembles. Through Katz's persuasion with the heads of the label, tensions began to ease a bit, and their long cherished notion of recording "The Art of the Fugue" was finally approved. That, along with "The Mozart Album" were the last projects the Canadian Brass recorded for CBS (which had become Sony Classics by that time through the purchase of the label by the giant Japanese corporation). Although relations between the group and the label had begun to run more smoothly, an unexpected turn of events was on the horizon.

The Brass had originally signed with CBS in 1983, and the contract ran until 1989. By the time negotiations were underway for the contract renewal at CBS, Gunther Breest, formerly at Deutsche Grammophon, had taken over as head of the label. The Brass was most unhappy with the contract as offered, and the negotiations extended over many months. In the meantime, an old friend of the Canadian Brass, Costa Pilavachi, was in a remarkable career transition. For a few important years in the 1970s Costa had been the Brass' manager in Canada. Later he had moved to the Boston Symphony, serving as Seiji Ozawa's artistic adminstrator, as well as running the summer Tanglewood Festival. Dr. Hans Kinzl, respected head of the Philips Classics label, had apparently observed Costa's work in the Boston Symphony's recordings on Philips. A position as head of A & R at the label became open, and Kinzl hired the young man from Boston. That set the stage for a dramatic turn of events in the Canadian Brass' recording career.

June, 1989. Canadian Brass was playing a series of concerts in Toronto with brass players from the Boston Symphony and the New York Philharmonic as their guests. Costa Pilavachi came to Toronto with his players from Boston, and confidentially told the Brass the news about his new job at Philips, which had not been announced and would begin in September. He asked the Brass: "By the way, where are you in your negotiations with Sony Classics?" The answer: "11th hour, 59th minute. Things are finally getting ironed out, but we don't actually have a contract in hand today." Costa asked them to do nothing for two days, and in that time called his future boss at Philips about their interest in the Canadian Brass. Philips was losing the Boston Pops, ironically enough, to Sony Classics, and Costa had been alerted that one of the priorities was to find a crossover artist to replace them. The next day Philips replied that they'd be most interested in signing the Brass. In record time for such a transaction, just over a week, the Brass' lawyers had in hand the general outline of the Philips contract. Costa had signed a major artist for a label where he wouldn't officially work for another two months. And with their old friend and supporter as head of A & R, and an eager and interested new international record label, the Canadian Brass felt it had a new lease on life. Gene notes that the move to Philips has been advantageous for several reasons:

top: Listening to Gabrieli/Monteverdi playback.
bottom: September 1990 recording of "Red, White and Brass," with New York and Boston players, conducted by Lukas Foss (right of Gene), Methuen, Massachusetts.

It makes all the difference in the world to be working with people who are supportive and extremely interested in the group's career. Also, Philips is very strong in Europe and Japan, both of which were places where we previously felt that our albums were not being adequately distributed. It was particularly frustrating because we have done a lot of touring in Japan and Europe, and have developed an awareness of the Canadian Brass in those markets, but never had the international sales that we felt were possible. That picture's changing now with Philips. Another interesting bonus is that the parent company of Philips is a leader in developing technology in ventures like High Definition Television. Philips organized and engineered a television special that we did, produced by Rhombus Media with Thames Television in London, that is the first classical project on HDTV, and also the first laser disk on HDTV. It's very exciting.

At this writing four albums have been released by Philips: an all-Beethoven project for triple brass quintet, including the Fifth Symphony and the Egmont Overture, "The Christmas Album," with the Elmer Iseler Singers once again guests of the Brass, "The Essential Canadian Brass," newly recorded favorites that actually formed the basis of the previously mentioned laser disk, and "Red, White and Brass." The latter is an interesting collection of "Americana" material in triple brass quintet arrangements. Members of the Boston Symphony and the New York Philharmonic were guests on the album, conducted by Lukas Foss, who was excited to be doing the first "pop" project of his career. Two further albums have been recorded: an all-Wagner album conducted by Edo De Waart, recorded in Berlin with guests from the Berlin Philharmonic and the Bayreuth Festival Orchestra, and an album of early jazz material arranged by Luther Henderson. There are many more albums in various stages of planning. Some are closer to becoming realities than others, but the nature of a recording career is to be constantly flirting with ideas, juggling them around; then after a great deal of consideration and planning only a few of them might get recorded. But you must have lots of ideas to start with. A rap album? A black gospel album? An album of French impressionist music? Lots of ideas have been discussed. There are always other artists around with which to collaborate on projects. There's talk of a possible gospel album, or a jazz album, or a project with an opera star like Kiri Te Kanawa or Jessye Norman. Brass Rap? With these guys anything's possible.

N. B.: A complete Canadian Brass discography appears in an appendix.

top: Paris, '73
middle: Hawaii, '78; Venice, '76
bottom: Berlin, '85; Japan, '79

ON THE ROAD... AGAIN

Morning in an Albuquerque café. David Ohanian leans back in his chair as he chats about touring with the Canadian Brass, slowly stirring his coffee. "We rarely sleep in the same bed two nights in a row." Pause. A surprised laugh. "Wait. I don't think I meant that the way it sounded. What I mean is, we rarely are in the same *city* two nights in a row."

It's hard to imagine how anyone could simply remain sane spending a third to a half of every year for the last twenty years out on the road, primarily playing one-night engagements, and still be healthy and in good humor. But that's exactly what the Canadian Brass has done. In a typical year they play concerts in over a hundred cities scattered around the globe: Warsaw, Los Angeles, Vancouver, Vienna, New York, Cologne, Rome, Washington, Peoria... the list goes on and on. It would be difficult to find an American, Canadian, Japanese, or German city where they haven't performed. Their concert schedule has taken them to Australia, the Soviet Union, China, throughout Europe, Asia, and the Middle East. While no records are kept about such things, it's probable that the Canadian Brass is the most traveled "classical" act in history. Discussing their jet age lifestyle, Gene casually mentions that they recently did a series of one-nighters in Bangkok—"One night getting there, one night to play, and one night getting back."

Just how has the Canadian Brass remained so happily together despite the constant pressures of twenty years of touring the world? Most important is that these five people love very much what they're doing. For more than two decades they've been able to maintain a friendly, supportive relationship among five creative egos, which in itself is an admirable accomplishment. The most prominent reason a majority of musical ensembles fail to maintain a career is that after a certain point the individuals simply can't get along. Just the fact that these men, all talented individuals with many career options available at any time, have stayed together so long is amazing, especially to other musicians. One professional violinist observes, "When I consider that in the space of the last twenty years I've been in more ensembles than I can remember, and that they've had this same group together all that time, I can't believe it. And four of the five have been there the whole time! I wonder if they know how lucky they are. I'd give a lot to be in a group that cohesive and supportive."

Even positive, gregarious people like Chuck, Ron, Fred, David and Gene admit that the concert schedule can sometimes take its toll. Gene points out, "I really believe that most people in the world would be miserable in the kind of constant, fast-paced travel we do. It takes a certain kind of personality to enjoy living like this." David is the group's official "travel agent," overseeing the complex travel arrangements. He describes the typical day out on tour. "We often get up before dawn. We take the first flight out in the morning, connect in some city, and then land at the destination at about 1 or 2 o'clock in the afternoon. At the hotel we might grab a nap or relax a bit before eating a meal. Then it's to the concert site to set up, have a rehearsal, and do the show. The next day the cycle starts all over again. To have time for sightseeing or visiting friends is pretty rare." Fred adds, "You have to remember why you're there, and can't do anything that is going to deplete your energy or swerve your attention away from the performance."

In an age when an increasing number of performers view live concerts as a necessary burden to bear in order to promote record sales, it's unusual to find a group of musicians fiercely committed to performing night after night. It may surprise some to learn that even after over two thousand performances together, the Brass still rehearses diligently nearly every day, working on new material for concerts or recordings, as well as brushing up old favorites that they may have played hundreds of times. When not performing a concert in the evening, the day normally includes a three hour rehearsal begining at 11 A.M. For years they rehearsed at a picturesque old church in Toronto, but now since three members live in Florida and the other two live in New York, they are likely to be found rehearsing in either of those

144

THE CANADIAN
BRASS

top: Bumper Sticker
from the 70s. Thousands
were disappearing. The
Brass finally figured out
why— see right

CANADIAN
ASS

Touring Canada 1976.

places or in any city where they are performing. The rehearsal is a perfect balance of relaxation and concentration. Even most professional musicians don't play 100% full-out throughout a regular run-of-the-mill rehearsal the way these players do. That's particularly true of many brass players, who tend to tire easily. The members of the Canadian Brass seem to have long ago reached a level of endurance where it appears that they can play as long and as strenuously as they like without showing signs of wear. When asked if they rehearse at this level every day, they don't even seem to understand the question. Another observation becomes clear in these daily sessions. Audiences the world over have seen plenty of proof that these five men love to perform. It becomes apparent in rehearsal that they also share a pure pleasure in making music together, even with no audience present. (Although with even one spectator in the room they can't help but play to the "audience.") Every musical detail is discussed with an easy familiarity, reminiscent of a casual conversation between brothers over dinner at home, and any disagreement dissolves quickly.

Their concertizing takes them to smaller cities or to the world's premiere concert halls. A particularly important step for the Brass was their first performance at Carnegie Hall on April 22, 1980. It was not only a milestone for them, but for brass quintets in general. Never before had a brass ensemble played a concert in this legendary shrine of music. The players knew it was risky, and there was some understandable apprehension within the group. Ron and Fred had spent several years as free-lancers in New York, and knew full well what an unsuccessful debut at Carnegie could do to the prospects of an ensemble. It could have a permeating effect on future bookings, on concert fees, on recording contracts, and the prospects for playing other major halls around the world. To fail in such an undertaking would also undoubtedly be personally very painful. But finally, unanimously persuaded that it was the right challenge, the quintet forged ahead, resulting in a resounding critical and popular success. That debut can be viewed as carrying far-reaching implications beyond just the career of the Canadian Brass. Here was proof that, for the first time ever, a brass ensemble could hold the stage in the toughest, most

146

Carnegie Hall

SEASON1979-1980 SEASON

Tuesday Evening, April 22, 1980 at 8:00

GURTMAN AND MURTHA
present

The Canadian Brass

FREDERIC MILLS, *Trumpet* GRAEME PAGE, *French Horn*
RONALD ROMM, *Trumpet* EUGENE WATTS, *Trombone*
CHARLES DAELLENBACH, *Tuba*

10TH ANNIVERSARY CONCERT

SAMUEL SCHEIDT (1587-1654)	Galliard Battaglia
G.F. HANDEL (1685-1759) (arr. F. Mills)	Suite from "Water Music" Allegro vivo—Air/Hornpipe— Allegro maestoso
HENRY PURCELL (1659-1695) (arr. F. Mills)	Sonata for Two Trumpets Maestoso—Adagio—Presto
GIOVANNI GABRIELLI (1557-1612)	Canzona Prima a Cinque
J.S. BACH (1685-1750) (arr. F. Mills)	Toccata and Fugue in D minor
Arr. by LUTHER HENDERSON	Fats Waller Suite

Intermission

Lighting by David Hignall

This concert is supported in part by
the **Canadian Consulate General** in Nev~

Management:
KAZUKO HILLYER INTERN'
250 West 57tⁿ
New York. '

The Canadian Brass's ?
specially designe~

The Canadian Brass r~

The photographing or sound recording of any perform
or sound recording inside this theater without the wri~
Offenders may be ejected and liable fo

Carnegie Hall debut—the first brass ensemble ever to play there.

147

discriminating performing arena in the world, filling the house and satisfying important critics just as surely as the best orchestras and most famous solo performers. It was heady stuff, and once the Brass had a dose of it, they couldn't resist going back for more.

In the 1985-86 season the Canadian Brass went so far as to book a series of four different concerts at Carnegie Hall in the space of just six months. This was a very bold move with many risks. It's one thing to do a concert in New York every year and a half or so, but quite another to pull off four successive appearances within such a brief time span. Were there enough interested concert-goers in the city to fill the hall four times over? Continuing their Midas touch, the Brass sailed through it with huge success. One concert was a particular triumph, an afternoon performance on Superbowl Sunday, January 26, 1986. Chuck tells the story.

> In a place like Carnegie Hall there are only so many choice dates available within a concert season. You're competing for dates with all the top orchestras in the world, as well as with celebrity performers from Kiri Te Kanawa to Frank Sinatra. Booking four concerts in one season multiplied the problem to a far greater extent, and we reluctantly had to take a booking on the afternoon of the Superbowl, wondering if anyone at all would show up. We've always felt that our real competition for drawing audiences doesn't come from other musical performances, but from things like the circus, the Ice Capades, movies, television, and certainly from athletic events. And here we were, up against the biggest sporting event of the year! We were elated when they told us we had sold out rather easily, but the biggest compliment was yet to come. On the day of the concert our manager, Jimmy Murtha, had the experience of being offered tickets at an inflated price by a scalper out on 57th Street. What a high compliment! To have the scalpers working your concert at Carnegie Hall, while the Superbowl is being played to the largest television audience of the year!

Superbowl Sunday has been a lucky day for the Brass more than once. That also turned out to be the day of their debut on another legendary American concert stage, Orchestra Hall in Chicago. They began that Sunday morning in Indianapolis, having played a concert there the previous night. The entire midwest had been hit hard with severe winter weather, and it was soon discovered that all flights out of Indianapolis had been cancelled. The Brass spent a hectic and desperate couple of hours trying to figure out how to get to Chicago for the important afternoon performance.

top: Australia, '81
middle: London, '80
bottom: Saudi Arabia, '78

149

In all their years together they had never once cancelled an appearance for any reason, and were determined this would not be a first. At last they found a pilot who was willing to fly them to Midway Airport in a small private plane. Even that didn't entirely solve the travel problems. Upon landing they soon discovered that, due to temperatures at -15° and blinding blowing snow, most of the city's taxis had stopped running. After some anxious waiting they found one lone cab, which had to make two trips from the airport to Orchestra Hall in order to transport all the bags, bodies and instruments. They arrived backstage in just enough time to change clothes and quickly warm up. Knowing that the audience would be subject to the same obstacles they had themselves faced, it was realistic to expect that the attendance would be sparse and the much anticipated date a fiasco. In disbelief and grateful amazement they looked out from the stage to a cheering full house. Another unlikely triumph.

As if being the first chamber group to tour China wasn't enough, the Canadian Brass also toured the Soviet Union at the height of the Cold War, and have been back since to see the revolutionary changes there. "Russian audiences are extremely extroverted," stated Ron. "They love the performing arts in a very passionate way there that is rather unique. I think we played six encores there for one concert—they just wouldn't let us leave."

In one of the oddest circumstances yet, the Brass was invited back to Moscow to play for the opening of the first McDonald's in that country, truly a sign that the Cold War was over and decadent Western capitalism had arrived. The fellows played a concert for Russian and McDonald's officials and guests in, of all places, the Kremlin. (Tell me times haven't changed!) In keeping with the wackiness of the adventure, they happened to run into Buddy Hackett in the Kremlin—hey, it makes as much sense as the rest of the trip. At the actual opening of (by now) the world's most famous hamburger stand, there were literally thousands and thousands of people trying to get in. In bitter Moscow cold, when their lips weren't sticking to the mouthpieces, they played street performances for the hungry Russians, and eventually got a bite of those glasnost burgers themselves.

First Soviet tour, above, 1978; most recent, below, 1990. They certainly look more prosperous, don't they?

above:
Buddy
Hackett—
Live from
the Kremlin

middle:
Playing for
the thousands
waiting to get
into the Moscow
McDonald's,
opening day,
1990

bottom:
Those Moscow
Macs aren't bad

In a general interview about touring, the conversation bounces around from player to player, like some off-beat, five-sided verbal tennis match:

— Do you remember Singapore? I know we played there, but I can't remember a thing about it.
— It must have been summer, because all I know is that it was incredibly hot. Why couldn't we have gone in the spring when the weather was better?
— No, no. That *was* the spring.
— Well, it sure felt like summer to me.
— We were there for a press conference with Air Canada because they were launching a new route there or something.
— And we were outside trying to play in a 90° steam for this TV crew that was taping us...
— I was sweating so much that the mouthpiece kept sliding all around my face.
— Now I remember...

To an outside observer it might seem that all the quick travel could become a blur. It can. Gene has said, "The thing about all those travel jokes like 'if this is Tuesday this must be Cleveland' is that after a while they're too true to be very funny." However, once the Brass gets started on a roll in discussing their life on the road, they come up with one detailed story after another. For instance...

Gene: "In the early years of the group we played a 28-concert tour of Saskatchewan, and we didn't even play the two large cities! Needless to say, we had a problem finding places to eat in all these small towns, because sometimes the best restaurant around would be the Shell station on the corner. We went together into a grocery store one day in a small town somewhere wanting something to munch on. Each one of us wound up buying a huge bag of puffed wheat that I remember was on sale for $1.70. I mean, these were five gigantic bags of the stuff! When we came out on stage to play the concert that night, we heard someone whispering in the audience, 'Hey look, those are the nuts who bought all that puffed wheat today!' It had already gone all over town."

left: Backstage at intermission
right: I think you've got the wrong
head, David.

Chuck continues: "It really *is* a problem eating sometimes. Years ago we were in France, and Gene was having trouble deciphering a menu. At last he seemed to recognize enough words to order what he wanted, which included some type of *fromage*. He was very surprised when the waiter brought him a big plate of head cheese! That reminds me of another food story about Gene. Back in the early days, when we were playing hundreds of school performances, Gene had a ritual of beginning every day by finding the best doughnut shop around. He'd always get these enormous, Texas-sized apple fritters. The funny thing was that he was a vegetarian at the time. Can you imagine a vegetarian starting every day with a huge hunk of deep fried sugar and fat! In all fairness I should tell you that he doesn't eat like that anymore."

David begins this story, and Ron jumps in to finish it:

"One September we started the first tour of a new concert season. The first date happened to be in Wabash, Indiana. We flew into Indianapolis, and the airline lost all our bags—all five of us at once! We had arranged to have someone pick us up and drive us to Wabash. So here we are, traveling very light, without our suits for the concert that night. It turned out that the driver's wife knew someone who ran a formal shop, so he called ahead to her, and she called to keep the shop open, because normally they closed early on Saturdays. We finally got there, and spent a hectic hour debating about what to rent for the concert, everybody having their own ideas about what would look good. We finally settled on these silvery looking things. I guess we thought that the audience could relate to them, because they had probably just seen them at a prom or a wedding or something. We thought we looked pretty slick that night."

Lost luggage has happened on many other occasions, but not to the entire group at once. Each player has had to face the prospect of playing a concert in his street clothes on at least one occasion—four guys in blue tuxes with white tennis shoes, and one guy in jeans and cowboy boots. The Brass decided long ago that when this happens that they simply wouldn't make any comment about it to the audience (which is far funnier than any joke they could ever come up with about the situation). Ron was the innocent victim for an afternoon concert in New Jersey. He played the first half of the concert in his jeans. By the intermission the airline had delivered the lost bag, so a relieved Ron donned his blue outfit and matched the other four for the second half. Strange as it may seem, not one person from the audience said a word about it afterwards. Ron speculates, "Either they were fast asleep, or they were so moved by the performance that they didn't notice. Or maybe they just sat there thinking 'those Canadian Brass—what a bunch of cards.'"

An episode happened to Fred Mills while on tour involving a missing bag. But this time the bag wasn't lost—it was stolen. As Fred relates: "We had played a concert in Paris in November of 1989, and were at Charles de Gaulle Airport going on to Germany. I stepped away from our luggage cart for about ten seconds, and when I turned around one of the bags was gone. It happened to be my bag that I always keep with me when traveling, because it had my passport, my wallet, my credit cards, my mouthpieces, our music for concerts, and our group petty cash of about $2000. What a mess! We got the music faxed to us that we needed, and I borrowed a mouthpiece or two. But the real problem was being in the middle of a European tour with no passport. I filed the theft with the French police, and they gave me an official paper showing that my passport had been stolen. That got me on the flight to Frankfurt, but the German police delayed me there, and the other guys had to go on without me on the connecting flight to Stuttgart. I finally got on a train to Karlsruhe, and then took a taxi from there to Stuttgart. They actually had to go ahead and play with just the four of them. I arrived just in time to see the guys getting a standing ovation at the end of the performance. It kind of made me wonder if there was something they weren't telling me! (laughs) I got my passport replaced with the help of the Canadian consulate in Munich. I remember playing a concert in Vienna on those strange, borrowed mouthpieces. It was no fun."

Listening to Fred tell this story, Ron interjects: "That performance in Stuttgart without Fred was a strange experience. I would play my part, and then there would be all this empty space where

Fred's part should be. So I jumped in and played everything I could remember. It was kind of like having a conversation with yourself or something. After all of that, I wish that we could say that we've learned our lesson, and now never let our bags out of sight for one second when we travel. But, of course, that's not quite true."

Another theft happened when Marty Hackleman was playing with the quintet in the mid 1980s. Just minutes before a concert in South Carolina he realized that his French horn had been stolen. The Brass went out onstage, asking the audience, "Is there a French horn in the house?" Sure enough, a fellow came forward with a horn for Marty to use for the concert. A week later the horn was returned, and with it came a bizarre story. The kid who stole the horn sold it for $15 to a sailor on board a banana boat bound for Panama. The thief was driving home in his car when he heard the story on the radio, and learned that there was a reward for the return of the distinctive French horn with a Canadian maple leaf on the bell. He immediately high-tailed it back to the sailor, offering to buy the horn back for $20. The captain of the boat overheard the two men in conversation, figured out what was going on, and called the police. Not a very bright thief, to ask only $15 for a French horn worth thousands!

There have been other occasions when the Canadian Brass has had to quickly come up with an instrument in order to proceed with a performance. Odd as it might seem, this doesn't worry them much. As Fred puts it, "Wherever we are, we can always find an instrument to play in an emergency. What is irreplaceable in what we do is the music itself. We never pack the parts we perform from in checked baggage." The players also know from experience that there are usually brass players attending their performances who have instruments nearby, and that knowledge has saved them at times, as in the instance of the stolen French horn.

It happened again in December of 1990 when they played an impromptu performance at the annual Midwest Band and Orchestra Clinic in Chicago, an annual event for teachers from around the country in the field of instrumental music education.

The Edinburgh
Festival, 1980

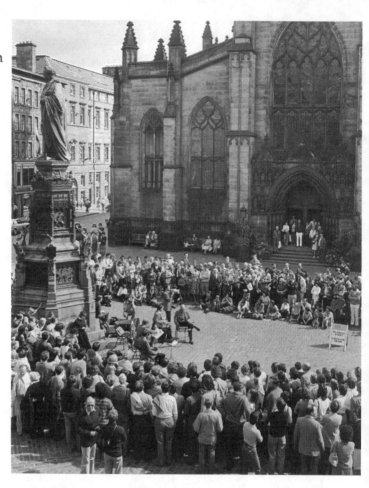

With Dizzy
Gillespie
in Edinburgh

The Brass happened to be flying through O'Hare that day and decided to drop in at the Chicago Hilton to play a casual performance as a Christmas present to all the musicians in attendance at the convention. The word spread quickly that afternoon about the rumored appearance, and by the time the Brass showed up, the atrium of the hotel was full to overflowing with a waiting audience of several hundred people. There was only one hitch. Just before they went on, Gene suddenly realized that he didn't have his trombone with him. No problem. He casually asked a group of people close at hand, "Does anyone have a trombone I could borrow for a few minutes?" By the tone of his voice the question might well have been, "Could you pass the salt, please?" A trombone quickly arrived. On with the show. No big deal.

One of the Canadian Brass' most pleasant recollections is playing at the Edinburgh Festival in 1980. The annual event is perhaps the most concentrated flurry of musical activity in the world, with hundreds and hundreds of performances scheduled within a few short weeks. The Brass played a full concert, but what they remember especially fondly were the informal performances they gave late in the evening after the conclusion of the day's scheduled events. Most of the musicians present at the festival would gather at a pub, and beginning at about 11 p.m. the Brass played for about an hour. It was like a happy, private club of kindred spirits from all over the world who all quickly became fans of the Canadian Brass.

As Gene often has said in performances, "The difference between a regular concert and a command performance for royalty is that for the command performance you don't get paid." The Canadian Brass have had more than one chance to find out. They first played for Queen Elizabeth at an airport reception in Canada in 1977, and have since played again for HRH and Prince Philip, for "Fergie" and Andrew, for Charles and Diana, and a few less glamorous European monarchs. "The Saints' Hallelujah," a brilliant juxtaposition of the "Hallelujah Chorus" ("one of the queen's favorites") and "When the Saints Go Marching In" ("one of our favorites") was written by Luther Henderson for them to play for an appearance before the queen of England. One royal

top: Command Performance for Queen Elizabeth and Prince Philip, 1975; Canadian Prime Minister Pierre Trudeau looks on (far right).
bottom: Receiving Prince Andrew, 1987.

performance occurred while the Brass was touring Australia. They were asked to take part in a concert featuring an eclectic mix of performers from several commonwealth countries, including musicians and dancers in tribal garb and bone-pierced noses. There were so many performers in the receiving line before the concert that the organizers put everyone in two rows, and the Brass were disappointed to find themselves in the back row. The disappointment didn't last. Prince Philip spotted them there, recognized Ron from previous performances, and being an apparent fan, made a bee line straight to the Brass for a nice long chat. In another royal receiving line incident, Duchess "Fergie" looked at Gene with his trombone and asked, "Isn't that awfully heavy?" Gene was somewhat bewildered at this unlikely question, the trombone being one of the lightest instruments to carry. In response he offered the princess a try, and being a good sport, she amused all by toying with the trombone.

More Canadian Brass touring anecdotes:

This is the sort of typical experience that might happen to a group performing in a small Canadian city. "We were touring with a semi-theatrical piece of music which needed unusual lighting. We'd made our request to the concert sponsors for the equipment required, and must have mentioned something about needing two 'barn doors,' which is a theatrical term for the shades used to focus the lighting. When we arrived at the hall to set up before the performance, this woman kept apologizing profusely about not being able to assemble all that we had requested, saying that they'd only been able to come up with one 'barn door.' We couldn't figure out what she meant, until we walked backstage and saw, leaning against a wall, a real barn door they had dragged in from some farm somewhere. We howled, of course! It was hilarious, and kind of sweet, too, that they had gone to such great lengths to try and fill what they must have thought was a bizarre request."

Being a Canadian based group, it was natural that the Canadian Brass was asked to play as part of the festivities for the 1976 Montreal Olympic Games. They played a concert in the athletes' village, but the appearance was far from thrilling. "When we stopped to think about it, we realized that the audience was comprised entirely of athletes who had lost their events and had been eliminated from competition. Anyone still in the running was off training somewhere. So the crowd was somewhat subdued, to say the least." The quintet was also asked to play at the Calgary Winter Olympics in 1988. They remember that there were hours of complicated rehearsals for the TV coverage. After all that, they were on for about two minutes of the broadcast. That's show-biz.

German audiences always eagerly look forward to the return of the Canadian Brass—their appearances there always seem to precipitate momentous historical events. In 1989 the Brass' playing brought down the Berlin Wall. In 1990 Helmut Kohl announced German reunification during the Brass' tour. In 1991 their German concerts launched Operation Desert Storm. And in 1992 Hans Dietrich Genscher resigned during a Canadian Brass concert tour. Germans can't wait for the 1993 tour.

You think that playing in a brass quintet isn't dangerous? Once, during a concert at the University of Massachusetts the Canadian Brass almost lost a tuba player. The guys were backstage during intermission, dressed in costumes for their cowboy opera for brass by Peter Schickele, *Hornsmoke*. As a special honor to their visitors, the brass players at the university played a thrilling arrangement of "Dies irae" from the Verdi *Requiem* from the back of the hall during intermission. Being in costume, the Brass stayed backstage behind the curtain listening to this special tribute. They were so moved by the students' performance that they wanted to show their appreciation in some way. Gene went up to the opening in the curtain and just put his hands through and applauded. Seeing this, Chuck thought he would rush over and do the same. He must have been running at pretty near top speed, because not only did his hands go through the curtain opening, but being unable to stop, his whole body sailed right through head first. The curtain happened to be at the very edge of the stage, so there was no place for Chuck to go but down a seven foot drop, sprawling on the first row of seats. (Luckily, no one was sitting there.) At that time his costume for *Hornsmoke*, playing the part of a parson, was a black robe with a gigantic

top: Tanglewood, 1986
with Seiji Ozawa

middle: Tanglewood, 1989
with Leonard Slatkin

bottom:
St. John the Divine,
New York City, 1989

white cross all down the back, so all the audience saw was this odd looking cross flying through the air. It was quite a fall. He was stunned, but not injured. Gene, who had seen this happen, reached through the curtain and pulled Chuck through in a kind of a crawl. He played the second half with a few bruises, but otherwise was perfectly fine. A fellow in the audience remarked on it afterwards. "We didn't know exactly what had happened. It looked like a sack of potatoes had been thrown through the curtain. And then, like the ascension, the sack of potatoes rose with a white cross on it and disappeared." Another observer expressed his opinion to the Brass, saying, "We thought it was part of your act that we just didn't get."

One of the most notorious Canadian Brass anecdotes goes back to the 1977 tour of China. Upon their arrival there, Gene Watts realized that he had failed to bring along a trombone mute that he needed. The Chinese hosts were very accommodating, and though there couldn't have been many trombones or trombone players in China at that time, they quickly located a very worn but usable, oddly-colored green trombone mute. Gene used it throughout the tour, but having plenty of far superior mutes at home, and not wanting to pack it in his bag for the return trip, he simply left the green mute in the hotel room upon leaving the country. At that time the Chinese were completely unaccustomed to having official foreign guests from the West. The hosts had tried hard throughout the tour to be as helpful as possible, so that whenever the Brass would leave discarded trash in the hotel rooms, it would be forwarded to them a few days later in another city. The Chinese just assumed that these were items that had been left mistakenly, and thought they were justly returning them to the rightful owners. This hilarious bit of cultural miscommunication became a running gag of the tour, and the entourage from Canada soon found themselves in the silly predicament of carrying around unwanted trash with them throughout the rest of the tour. About a year after the China trip, following a performance in Toronto, a gentleman walked up to Gene and said, "I recently had meetings with Chinese diplomats, and they asked me to give this to you." The man handed Gene a small package which turned out to be—you guessed it—the green Chinese trombone mute.

In the years since receiving this "long lost" mute, this has been Gene Watts' favorite anecdote, one that he has told to hundreds of people all over the world. But there's a part of the story that Gene has never known. Upon leaving the hotel that final day in China in 1977, Chuck spotted the much discussed mute in Gene's room. After having had their unwanted refuse forwarded to them all over China, Chuck quickly realized that here was the opportunity for some kind of practical joke. He quietly kept the mute hidden away for a year. Then, in the least likely situation, he chose a very unsuspicious accomplice for the high jinks in an absent-minded, professorial Canadian composer. Chuck coached him on just what to say, and innocently stood by and watched his masterful joke unfold as the man presented Gene with the mute. For the fifteen years since, every time he has heard an unsuspecting Gene tell the tale about the hyper-dutiful Chinese and their return of the discarded trombone mute, Chuck has always laughed just a bit harder than anyone else. The elaborate Daellenbach plot was the perennial source of so much rich, secret pleasure that he was never able to bring himself to confess to Gene the true story. Even at this incredibly late date he still hasn't told him, nor has anyone else. And reader, we entreat *you* not to spill the beans.

MEDIA MATTERS — RADIO, TELEVISION, & CRITICS

In this quick tour of Canadian Brass media matters it may be easy to see just how much media does matter.

RADIO

It's really no surprise that the Canadian Brass seems to have had a sense of media from the very beginning. The first formal concert they ever gave, in 1971, was actually broadcast over CBC radio. At the time CBC had a mandate to produce a large amount of indigenous Canadian programming, and the Brass was a natural—a variety of music and shtick to boot. There were several different commercial radio shows in Canada on which the quintet appeared in the early 70s, most prominent among them was a popular morning show called "This Country in the Morning," a national program with host Peter Gzowski. The impact of regular appearances on shows like this served as an effective entrée in introducing the group to many people. In fact, the Brass was able to begin booking concerts all over Canada largely due to their radio following. A few years later, it was an appearance on New York's WQXR that led to the Brass' introduction to RCA and their first major label recording contract—all because the right person was listening at the right time. Because the Brass has recorded so many albums of such diversity, they are a natural and regular programming choice for a variety of radio formats, including a live performance with Garrison Keillor on his "Prairie Home Companion." As a result, around the world millions of people hear the Canadian Brass at some point every day in many different countries, from Germany to Japan to Australia to Norway to you-name-it. In a world obsessed with television, it's easy to forget the power of good old-fashioned radio play.

top: Gene and Fred are a bundle of nerves before a live TV appearance in a Toronto studio, early 1970s. *bottom:* In the studios of WXQR in New York City with Bob Sherman, 1978— the appearance that led to the RCA contract

TELEVISION

The Canadian Brass may not be a household TV name along the order of Dobie Gillis or Mr. Magoo, but the tube has often called and the Brass has answered in a variety of ways. In the early years there were regular appearances in Toronto, particularly on daytime talk/variety shows. Guest appearances on prime time Canadian shows soon followed. Hello "Sesame Street," "CBS Sunday Morning," "The Today Show," and "Good Morning America." The Brass has made several appearances on the American morning shows over the years—including one on "The Today Show" on Christmas Day, 1990, when Bryant Gumbel, Joe Garagiola, Willard Scott and Deborah Norville tried to join them in playing a carol. The emphasis is on "tried" here. It's a good thing those folks are good at other things instead of brass playing.

There was a series of four half-hour Canadian Brass specials on CBC in the mid 1980s. It should have been a terrific experience with wonderful results, but somehow something went amiss in the way the shows were put together. To their dismay, the Brass lost creative control, and rather than just letting the Canadian Brass be the Canadian Brass, the CBC staff dreamed up elaborately overproduced production numbers, corny scripts and skits, with ridiculously juiced-up laugh tracks. Watching some of the numbers in those shows, it's hard to imagine just what the producers' aims were. Sometimes it looks as if they are trying to make MTV influenced "classical" videos, and the result is often just as scattered and incoherent as a run-of-the-mill rock video. Even the make-up is overdone. Watching the tackiest and most garish number in the four show series, you can just imagine the conversation among the producers. "What these guys need is more sex appeal. Anyone got any ideas? How about if we bring on a bunch of skimpily clad dancing girls and have them do some sort of routine while the guys are standing there with the horns. You know, the girls could just kind of bounce around and do anything really. You know how big aerobics are these days..." It's the funniest number in the four shows, but it's purely unintended humor. These five great musicians who have toured the world, played Carnegie Hall to the Hollywood Bowl, played for kings and heads of state, and been bestowed with every type of honor are treated like mere stage props.

Needless to say, the Brass was unhappy with the CBC specials, believing that the shows were bad enough to negatively affect their Canadian image for a couple of years. The ironic thing is that the CBC is constantly swimming in financial trouble. So what did they do? Spend about ten times what was necessary, and in the process make some less than great television.

Luckily, the Brass were able to make other television specials with much happier results. "Canadian Brass Live" is representative of a normal, everyday, extraordinarily entertaining Canadian Brass concert. No dancing girls or production numbers—just the guys, the music, their concert antics, the audience, and the resulting magic. Broadcast in the U.S. over PBS, the program was also released as a video for purchase. The show was honored by the American Film and Video Association Awards. In reviewing the video, *The Washington Post* had this to say:

> From their entrance down the main aisle playing 'Just a Closer Walk,' to their encore, an improbable combination of 'When the Saints Go Marching In' and Handel's 'Hallelujah Chorus,' this quintet of artists created an atmosphere of total enjoyment in which laughter freely mingled with gasps of amazement...It's amazing to watch what a rollicking good time these five talented people have while performing.

To North American eyes, some of the quintet's most interesting television appearances have been on Japanese TV. Chuck actually does pretty intelligible (one guesses) shtick in Japanese. Well, at least the audience laughs. The Brass is extremely popular in Japan, and tapes of their prime time appearances there in front of live audiences are fascinating proof of the universal appeal of entertaining and beautiful music.

The Canadian Brass had the unique distinction (?) of appearing on the very last "Merv Griffin Show." (How was it? "Well, Merv seemed kinda down that day.") Lots of other shows, among them Boston Pops, "Camera Three," a Smothers Brothers Comedy Special, and "Entertainment Tonight"—now *there's* a likely showcase for the world's great chamber ensembles! (The Brass

169

Two stills from the CBC specials of the 1980s.
above: As props for the dancing girls
below: Made up for the "Boy Mozart" number

were certainly the first.) A guest spot on a PBS special honoring Victor Borge came in 1990, along with another Canadian Brass special "On Stage at Wolf Trap," with guest star Judith Blegen of the Metropolitan Opera, which has been broadcast several times over PBS. (This is available for sale on video.) In 1989 Doc Severinsen was invited to play the national anthems at baseball's All-Star Game, held in Anaheim that year. Uncomfortable with the idea of playing the Canadian anthem, he would only accept the job if the producers brought the Canadian Brass in to play with him. Chuck recalls:

> Freddy quickly made some arrangements for us, and we made Doc look great, giving him the high, flashy stuff while we kept the tune going. It was a fun thing to do, but I can't say we wound up on camera much in the broadcast. All the cameramen were from 'The Tonight Show' and they were saying stuff like, 'Don't worry Doc, we'll give you lots of close ups. And who *are* those other guys anyway?'

In what is surely one of the most prominent brass concerts of all time, the Canadian Brass, along with two guest quintets comprised of players from the New York Philharmonic and the Boston Symphony, created a 1989 television program entitled "The Canadian Brass Spectacular." (It, too, is available for sale on video.) It's a feast for anyone who loves brass music, with fifteen of the best players in the world on one stage, displayed in a wonderful mix of repertory—from Gabrieli to "Beale Street Blues." This project was the natural outgrowth of several concerts and three recordings that the Brass initiated with these assembled forces, including what is now a legendary concert of Gabrieli and Monteverdi one Sunday afternoon at St. John the Divine in New York.

In 1991 the Brass again had their own TV special, this time initiated by Philips Classics and produced by Rhombus Media for worldwide distribution, entitled "Home Movies." The concept of the show, developed by director Niv Fichtman, featured young actors cast to be Chuck, Fred, David, Ron and Gene as young boys in a flashback approach, mixed in with the quintet in their real-life adult selves. The show is remarkable in the fact that it was the first "classical" program ever produced using the new process of High Definition Television (HDTV), and it will be the

left: With Oscar on the "Sesame Street" set

below: A Japanese television appearance

first laser disc release in that format (as well as on videotape).

But the biggest thrill of the quintet's television career, as Chuck relates, must have been appearing on "The Tonight Show" with Johnny Carson.

> You get there and you start asking yourself, 'I wonder how many times I've watched *The Tonight Show* in my life.' Then you start to think about how many millions of people could say the same thing, and then you realize that the same millions of people could be watching *you* tonight. Major goose bumps. It's almost like being in a museum. You're standing behind those famous curtains waiting to go on, and you go on stage and realize that you're standing on the star—Johnny's star—that marks his place for doing the monologue. It's a great thrill. All I could think at the time was, 'Don't screw up.'

MOVIES

Or rather, Movie. In 1987 the Canadian Brass got their first taste of what it was like to record a movie score, *The Couch Trip*, starring Dan Aykroyd, Walter Matthau, Charles Grodin and Donna Dixon. The film's director, Michael Ritchie, happened to hear the Brass with the L.A. Chamber Orchestra, and with the idea of using them for the movie, got in touch with the composer hired to do the film's score, Michel Columbier. It so happened that just the year before the Canadian Brass had commissioned a piece from this very same composer. The deal came together quickly. The only open window in the schedule was a three-day period in June, squeezed in at the end of a Japanese tour. In a very interesting article written by Chuck Daellenbach for the magazine *Canadian Musician*, he describes the experience of recording the score, and incidentally reveals some ideas about recording in general.

> First of all, we saw cuts of the film out of order, in the same way it is shot. If you like, it could be like shuffling pages of music and then playing the pieces in the new order. In the hands of the professionals such as we worked with though, very few problems were encountered. Columbier had scored each piece out, as with any recording session, the timing had been carefully worked out, and a click track kept us all on track and organized. Ritchie, a music co-ordinator whose responsibility it was to ensure the music was right for the film, and Columbier oversaw the entire process. At times Ritchie would call for a retake or

above: With "Couch Trip" composer Michel Columbier at a L.A. Chamber Orchestra premiere, 1987.
below: The 1989 All-Star Game in Anaheim, with Doc Severinsen and baseball's favorite players.

ask for a different feel musically for certain scenes, but the music as written basically suggested itself.

Very session oriented, our recording blocks were much tighter than we normally experience. Again, to achieve the specific results necessary, soundtrack recording needs such regimentation. Since we had always approached recording sessions with specific music written down and are all classically trained musicians, some of this process was second nature... Throughout the entire three-day event, we played to dozens of cues, completing between 40 and 70 minutes of music. It was our first experience of recording in Los Angeles and one which I personally went into a little dubiously, but emerged extremely impressed. In the past the Brass had always chosen to record in RCA's huge 1930s studio in New York or Toronto's St. Mary Magdalene church for the live, natural acoustic sound large spaces offer. Ideally, of course, I would love to record in a large concert hall such as Carnegie, but the expense is prohibitive. Studios, I had found, usually reduce the sound and rely on artificial reverb. Hats off to Frank Wolf at Group Four, the engineer who surpassed my expectations of any studio engineer. Wolf got a sound as good as any acoustic hall and changed my natural trepidation about studio recording...I admit it, I can't wait to see the film just to hear the final product of those sessions... In Ritchie we knew we had a contemporary director who didn't follow the current trend of inserting pop tunes into films, but focussed on the entire project through a score.

WRITERS AND REVIEWS

Short items and mentions, feature articles, and that friend and foe of all musicians, the review—people in the performing arts love to be written about (usually). "Features in magazines or Sunday papers are great," says Gene. "You get lots of columns or several pages, usually with pictures, and the best part is that you can count on the writer saying lots of nice things about us. I mean, just the fact that they chose to write an article about us is usually a pretty good sign that they like what we do." The Canadian Brass hits the newsstands in major publications around the world, in more languages than they can remember. "I like the stuff in foreign languages," comments Ron, "because you can imagine that it says whatever you like."

Bring up the subject of critics to any musician, and you're bound to get a mixed reaction. The Brass is no exception, but in fact has a great track record with the critics for over twenty years.

from the Ottawa *Citizen:*

A 'concert' by them is a hilarious mix of music and theatre—the sort of thing there's no real name for yet. Somebody has invented 'performance art,' but that's much too clumsy a phrase. They are brilliant brass players, whether they are spoofing or playing seriously.

from *The London Telegraph:*

The Rev. Sidney Smith is said to have described his idea of heaven as 'eating pate de foie gras to the sound of trumpets...' After hearing the Canadian Brass quintet I am inclined to share this notion with him—at least for the trumpets. In this case not only trumpets...were in evidence but also French horn...trombone...and tuba. These Five classically trained orchestral players made mincemeat of some of my prejudices in their first London appearance at the Queen Elizabeth Hall. I had never found either music or musical 'jokes' funny; some serious music could be ridiculous and most musical jokes were boring, but neither could be funny. I have never imagined that anyone could strike the exact note of high-level comedy in music as successfully as these five do, singly and in combination.

from *Newsweek:*

In what promises to be the beginning of a new golden age of brass, the flourish of classical brass can be heard once more. Dozens of brass chamber-music groups, mainly quintets...are challenging the dominance of the string quartet...the Canadian Brass has done more to popularize brass playing than any other group...In the oddest tribute of all, string players are now mimicking brass—at least in Canada, where one new string quintet is regaling audiences with transcriptions of the Canadian Brass' repertory.

from *The New York Times:*

Canadian Brass is an instrumental quintet, not a national personality trait...brilliant virtuosity and ensemble playing of remarkable unanimity. The Bach work, arranged by Frederick Mills, one of the two trumpeters, was a tour de force in the performance. In excerpts from Handel's 'Water Music,' also arranged by Mr. Mills, the ornaments were spectacularly handled.

from *Ovation:*

What works for the Canadian Brass, however, might not work for anyone else, because each artist has to build his own bridge of communication from stage to audience. The Brass build theirs with peerless performances, spontaneous humor and an inner spark that reaches out and creates a very special rapport.

from *The Cincinnati Post:*

...the Canadian Brass exhibited an unusual combination of technical polish and musical flair. While the Canadians have developed a serious reputation as an internationally recognized classical music ensemble, the quintet is unafraid to let its hair down...Romm's talents were showcased in a virtuoso interpretation of 'Carnival of Venice.' The performance brought back memories of an earlier time, when a trumpeter was equal to a tenor in the ability to dazzle an audience through florid passages and high notes.

from *The London Free Press:*

There's almost as much talk as music in the Brass' program. Watts and Daellenbach do most of the honors and both can deliver laughs. But don't let the laughs blur what is top-rate musical ability. These men have toured the world and put out album after album but their laurels rest not just on knocking classical music off its pedestal, but on mastering their instruments. Their playing is as golden as their horns.

from *The New York Post:*

The Canadians delivered... with a mixture of virtuosity and engaging showmanship which both educated and entertained...There was not a flat or slow-moving movement, no lapse in the capacity audience's attention and involvement. Just excellent musicianship and high-spirited, intelligent fun. It's an infectious combination.

from *The New York Times:*

The Canadian Brass, a quintet of lively young men who have built a following by being charming as well as by their excellent handling of wind instruments, gave a concert at Alice Tully Hall on Tuesday night that was a model of relaxed merriment.

from *The Washington Post:*

...neither playing while lying on the floor, nor imitating ballerinas in a marvelously witty Tribute to Ballet, nor negotiating the unbelievable technical feats of their arrangement of Bach's Toccata and Fugue in D Minor presented challenges these men couldn't meet.

from *The Birmingham Post* (England):

Chuck Daellenbach's description of the Toccata and Fugue in D Minor would not have disgraced the great Groucho himself for its inspired lunacy.

The Canadian Brass have that ideal blend and balance which should be the envy of all brass ensembles.

One of the world's greatest ensembles. All five men have an agility that comes close to the phenomenal, and they work at achieving a wide dynamic range that fills their music with lights and shadows.

Etcetera. Occasionally a critic just doesn't seem to get it. It's one thing for a writer to knock the performance because he didn't like the playing or the repertory—that happens to every musician once in a while. But there have been journalists who just aren't able to get their minds around a Canadian Brass concert. Chuck explains:

> Reviewers have to accommodate themselves to the brass quintet, and a few seem slow to do that. It's not a string quartet, it's not an orchestra, it's not an opera singer—it's a brass quintet. And from a concert standpoint, what cross section of music belongs to a brass quintet? We're not looking at original pieces by Beethoven or Haydn or whoever, because obviously they didn't write any brass quintets—they didn't have such a thing back them, not until the 1950s really. We can commission new pieces by living composers, and we've done a lot of that, but you can't build a concert that appeals to general audiences based on that because it's too specialized. So transcriptions are the key. We look for what music would sound best on our instruments, and that includes Bach as well as Dixieland. Once in a while someone has a narrow view of what a concert should be, and isn't comfortable with following Handel with Fats Waller, because in their mind, I suppose, we should be doing 'serious' classical repertory, and not what they consider pop music. Well, is an entire century now of varied styles of jazz and musical theater and film music and even rock, is all of that just considered pop music now and forever? And to be honest, when you look at the 'serious' repertory from this century it isn't nearly as rich, nor as interesting or compelling. Even the most progressive thinking academic musicologists are realizing these things. In a way, because we've always just treated music as music, and mixed it up from the start, we've been on the forefront of a progressive attitude about music. And O.K., I'll admit that we were just following our noses, and didn't approach it from any lofty philosophical vantage point. But we wound up with a concept of repertory that mirrors the thoughts of today's most radical ivory tower musicologists. Once in awhile a critic just isn't hip enough to get it, and they complain about

us not doing enough of a traditional concert or whatever. Luckily, that kind of thinking is in the very minor minority.

He touches on some fascinating thoughts. Indeed, the aesthetic tension between "popular" music and "serious" music is something that will probably continue to accelerate, potentially allowing for a new, eclectic aesthetic such as that practiced by the Canadian Brass. The traditional classical world, from the symphonies and opera companies to the conventional academic music programs at universities, continues to struggle with the whole concept of how to approach popular music, for they are no longer able to simply ignore it, which has been a prevalent attitude throughout the century.

In an excerpt from a review that ran in *The Seattle Times*, the writer more or less complained that the Canadian Brass performance wasn't enough of a "real concert." Among other statements displaying a suspicious attitude, the critic wrote, "And laugh the audience did, last night in the 5th Avenue Theater, where a rousing good time was had by a theater full of people inclined to applaud between movements of the few classical selections left on the Canadian Brass' program." Read between the lines and you'll find a twist on that old proverb: Prudishness is next to godliness.

A Japanese magazine cover from 1982.

PASSING IT ON—
A COMMITMENT TO
MUSIC EDUCATION

Despite up to 150 concerts a year and a demanding recording schedule, the Canadian Brass has always found time to nurture young musicians. Whether it be in school appearances, as in the 1970s, or in master classes, published educational music, videos, or their own line of instruments, the Brass has remained committed to fostering the same kind of positive musical experiences for others that they all remember getting themselves as children.

The dean of the group in this area, naturally, is Chuck, who comes qualified for the distinction with his Ph.D. in music education. Get him onto the subject, and he assumes the tone of a crusader:

"For so long in this century, American schools led the world in music education, and for everyone. Other countries have programs to cherry pick only those students who show remarkable talent, and the rest have no arts education at all. The U.S., on the other hand, has had a tradition of community-oriented band, orchestra and choral programs at all levels, and involved a healthy cross section of students. The serious musicians are encouraged by this, sure, but it also gives millions of people who are not headed toward a professional music career a broadening and fun experience in a music program. What we've seen in the last decade, especially, is a dramatic cutback in funding arts education. In an effort to increase the failing standards of education, the push has been focussed almost entirely on the 'core curriculum' to the exclusion and neglect of anything else. Somehow, the arts have been unaligned with the core, and have been viewed as a separate and expendable luxury. What we have to do is to realign music with the core curriculum, and there's every reason to do that. The positive effect of music on kids is so obvious to us that it's a real challenge to articulately persuade people of its importance, but that has become our task—and when I say 'our' I mean everyone concerned about the future of music in the schools. The tragedy seems most exaggerated in urban school districts plagued with lack of discipline, apparent student disinterest, racial tension, a general lack of community support, and a common lack of self-esteem among so many young people. We *know* that music could help solve those and other problems. Music is a vehicle for a student to identify his or her capabilities, to structure thinking, to learn social skills that he can't learn anyplace else, to accomplish something by working together with other people, and to generally feel better about himself. We've heard students tell us that they feel they have to practice and try their best in their bands or choruses because if they don't, more than anything else they'll be letting down their friends—not their parents, not their teachers, but the people sitting there in that band with them. That's a powerful thing to hear from a kid, and a testament to the feeling of responsibility and accomplishment that music can foster better than anything. The 'basic skills' of math, science and reading are individual oriented goal situations. Music, drama and sports are the only things in the schools with group goals and the resulting values that come from that. The arts are better even than sports in this regard, because you don't have to deal with the overt competitive edge—a winner and loser— and also music can involve far more people than a sports program. Everybody has the ability to be in a music program. There are no absolute achievements that apply. Sure, maybe some kids will never play Scriabin sonatas or Maynard Ferguson solos. So what? Maybe it's enough for them to reach a level of skill to play in church, or play pop music with their friends, or to be able to play in community bands or sing in choirs the rest of their lives. That's a lot to give someone, and it all starts in those formative years in school.

"And this is why music has to be part of a core curriculum. We need to articulate these things to people — to teachers, principals, administrators, legislators, and everyone involved in our communities. There are music educators attempting this very

With Japanese music students.

thing. As professional musicians, we think we can help spearhead the movement and call more attention to it, because of our visibility and our longstanding relationship with music education."

An instance in 1991 illustrates in a tangible way just what Chuck has said. An inner city Los Angeles high school is an example of how dramatic the challenges are for music programs in the U.S. The director told the Canadian Brass that the school's appropriated budget for music for the year was $0. He had about 30 kids in a band program, and the school owned exactly 8 brass instruments that all the children shared. The Brass presented a clinic with the students in that school, and were touched by their plight. The best player in the school didn't play in the clinic because there just wasn't a horn for him to play. They resolved to try and help them, and agreed to perform a benefit concert at the school. The Brass took no fee, and the school was able to keep whatever income they could raise from ticket sales.

While the quintet obviously cannot directly help all schools in the way they did in Los Angeles, this concept of "adopting" a school's music program is a powerful one. Imagine the effect on the public schools of North America if just a small percentage of successful professional musicians were to follow the example of the Canadian Brass.

The group's work hasn't been limited to American and Canadian schools. They've worked with students in Europe and Japan as well. David states:

> Those Japanese kids are incredibly regimented. You walk into a classroom and hear stone silence. Every chair is perfectly placed, with exactly the same distance between each one. Each kid sits perfectly still and erect, listening intently to whatever you tell them. They're very well prepared, and they play well. But for an American, I can't say it's entirely comfortable. When we did the clinic in L.A., for instance, the kids were hardly orderly—chairs were all over the place, and instrument cases lying open wherever. But the kids were excited and interested, and I guess that it felt much more a comfortable experience.

The Brass has had a direct link to school music in Walter Barnes, who runs a very successful band and orchestra program in the

top and bottom: Master class at the Moscow Conservatory,
November, 1990.

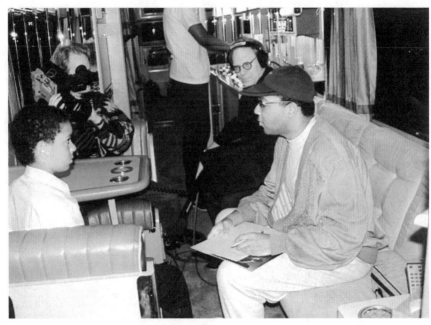

A scene from the video "The Canadian Brass Master Class," introducing a starstruck young trumpeter to Wynton Marsalis.

NEW ENGLAND CONSERVATORY OF MUSIC

THE PRESIDENT AND TRUSTEES
HAVE CONFERRED UPON

The Canadian Brass

The Degree of
Doctor of Music
honoris causa

GIVEN UNDER THE SEAL OF THE CONSERVATORY AT BOSTON IN THE COMMONWEALTH OF MASSACHUSETTS ON THE fifteenth DAY OF May IN THE YEAR OF OUR LORD ONE THOUSAND NINE HUNDRED AND ninety-two

PRESIDENT

CHAIRMAN OF THE BOARD

Honorary doctorates from the New England Conservatory of Music, 1992.

186

Toronto Public Schools. With Walter's students as beneficial guinea pigs, the Brass is able to try out their own ideas, specifically, about how to approach brass education. Walter has also worked extensively with the Brass on their publications, which brings us to another subject...

Almost without precedent in music publishing is the Canadian Brass' ambitious catalog of brass music, addressing the needs of students from beginning up to professional levels. Hundreds of titles have been released over the years. Hal Leonard Publishing is the group's music publisher, and Steve Rauch, a vice-president of that company, had this to say: "Being the world's largest publisher of printed music, we work with literally hundreds of artists of different kinds. Of all the major performers we work with, no one is as seriously and consistently interested in creating meaningful music publications as the Canadian Brass." Chuck, director of the publishing activities of the group states, "We've had to create, virtually from scratch, our own brass quintet repertory because so little existed before we began. At this point in history it looks as if the brass quintet is as established a musical medium as a string quartet or a woodwind quintet. But brass quintet literature is needed. We feel a responsibility to share this with other players." A few hundred titles from the group's vast library of music for quintet have been published exactly as recorded and performed by the Brass. Thus, any five players anywhere are able to study and play everything from "The Saint's Hallelujah" to the landmark transcription of "The Art of the Fugue." But the advanced and professional level players are not the only ones to benefit. There is a widely used series of books that presents graded repertory for brass quintets, along with playing tips and brief historical information about the music. The quintet even took the time to record all of this educational literature, giving students a guide to use in their studies. Teachers have found this series so useful that they began asking for the same kind of approach in teaching woodwinds and strings as well. And at this writing, the Canadian Brass, along with Hal Leonard, is planning the release of just such material.

The publications also include solo literature for each instrument,

Samples of Canadian Brass publications.

including recorded performances by the Brass, which reveals each player in great solo literature for his instrument — the Hadyn trumpet concerto, the Hummel concerto, the Mozart third horn concerto, the Rimsky-Korsakov trombone concerto, and a Magic Flute suite for tuba, among other titles. Another series of solos, with recordings by the Brass, have been released on the beginning, easy and intermediate levels.

In addition to publications addressing the needs of musicians and teachers, the Brass has also created videos on the subject. "The Canadian Brass Master Class," endorsed by MENC (Music Educators National Conference) is a best-selling program that shows the players informally discussing technical and aesthetic aspects of playing and performing, and working with student musicians. "Strings, Winds, and All That Brass: The Inspiration of Music" is a persuasive, truly inspirational video program that illustrates the Brass' support of music education, and is uniquely designed to motivate students or to persuade parents of the importance of their child's participation in an instrumental music program. In a charming highlight of the video, the Brass introduces a wide-eyed twelve-year-old trumpeter to his idol, Wynton Marsalis.

For years people have asked Chuck, Gene, Fred, Ron and David this question, "Do you know where I can get a good horn?" The quintet has always had its instruments designed for them. In the last couple of years they realized, "If we're already in the business of designing our own instruments, why don't we start our own line of trumpets, trombones, horns and tubas?" The Canadian Brass Collection was officially launched in 1991.

As can be easily seen from all this varied activity, the passionate cause of encouraging music among young people is something the usually anything-but-serious Canadian Brass takes very seriously. "North America has set a standard for the world in brass playing. For so long our culture has produced a staggering amount of great brass players in all styles. The whole world holds American brass playing as its highest standard. We just can't sit by and let that slip away from us."

THE FANS SPEAK

It seems fitting that this book concludes with a few highlights selected from mailbags of letters that the Canadian Brass is flattered to receive every year. Most of the letters are full of excitement over hearing a concert, or discovering albums or videos. For instance:

Dear Canadian Brass,

I want to say Thank You for the beautiful evening listening to you in concert. Incomparable how the different pieces were played. Four encores at the end, with a few minutes of standing ovation—this is proof of how much the audience enjoyed the music. I wish Canadian Brass the same success during their other performances in Germany, Austria and France. For any information concerning further concerts in Germany during the next years, and any new CD releases, I am thanking you very much…

(from Frankfurt, Germany)

Or this one:

Dear Canadian Brass,

While the memory of the concert still lingers in my mind and the music in my ears, I want you to thank—all five—for an event which I might remember to the very last day of my life. I am, more than you, grateful…

Yours truly,
(from Oslo, Norway)

(Hey, imagine what it would sound like if you tried to write a letter in Norwegian.)

Dear Chuck, David, Ron, Fred and Walter [sic],

I hope I didn't get the names wrong, but my heart's in the right place

191

(center chest cavity, slightly to the left), and I just wanted to thank you for the fine autographed photo that I recently received... I live far from a city and rarely can get to concerts, so I must depend on your recordings. If you never did anything but Basin Street you'd be a roaring success.

Blessings,
(from Mission, British Columbia)

Well, four out of five names isn't bad. Sorry, Gene.

Dear Frederick, David, Ronald, Eugene and Charles!

I just wanted to let you know that your recent performance here compelled me to write and let you know that while listening to you I had tears running down my face from laughing so hard. Thank you, thank you, thank you.

(from Greensboro, North Carolina)

The Brass thanks you, too—they think.

Dear Canadian Brass,

...Tonight you provided us with another wonderful evening at Wolf Trap—the sixth time we've seen you perform there or at Kennedy Center. Looking forward to number seven.

(from Washington, D.C.)

A large percentage of the mail comes from young fans, often from brass players:

Dear Members of the Canadian Brass,

We enjoyed your performance. It was funny and we learned alot. But not enough so we want you to come back. I liked it even when you started to act something out and someone else butted in and made everybody laugh. I am very interested in your act.

Yours truly,
(from a third grader in Burlington, Ontario)

Dear Canadian Brass,

I think your music was very good. You were also pretty funny and you explained the music good. I think other people will like you too. I would like to play the trumpet some day and maybe you could show me.

Dear Canadian Brass,

I am a great fan of yours. I admire your playing abilities and the way you make music fun... I am in the tenth grade and play the trumpet in the high school band and city youth orchestra. I have seen you live and I have all your tapes. I am planning on attending your concert in Kalamazoo in a few weeks...

From a budding Gertrude Stein:

Dear Canadian Brass,

You were just great everybody enjoyed your performance I learned a lot about music. I love music that's my favorite especially singing I think it was the trumpet that I liked best. You guys were just great you know you guys make a great team. Work hard and show everybody you can play also you were funny.
                              So long and love...
P.S. Come back

Dear Canadian Brass,

...My brother plays the trumpet at home and my dad loves it but my mom doesn't. I love the way you play and the jokes. I would like to know how many people are in the whole group. Thank you very much.

(Um... five, I think.)

Dear Canadian Brass,

...I like the music very much. I licked [sic] the jokes to...

The next letters are typical of those received in the early days of the group when they played performances in Canadian schools.

To the members of the brass quintet,

How are you and your funny stunts? You have a very good and funny group. Ronnie was really funny when he coppied [sic] what Gene said… You have a real good group and most of us had a great time to listen to your music and laugh at your jokes.

"*Most* of us"?

Dear Sirs,

I thank you very much. I like the joke alot. The trumpets were my best and the trumbone was my second best and the tuba was my third best and at last the French horn…

"Joke"?

Dear Members of the Brass Quintet,

You played wonderful in the gym. The best instrument was the French horn. I asked one man how much it costs and he said 1,000 dollars or 100 dollars and up. The tuba made a loud sound. You were very funny. Thank you for coming.

Dear Brass Quintet,

I have a few questions for you, please answer them if you write back. Is your group always funny when you perform?

There are letters from young brass players who have seen the Canadian Brass videos:

Dear Canadian Brass,

I really enjoyed and learned much from your new [Canadian Brass Master Class] video. Through your humour—both in your speech and music—you have led both the musically ignorant and music-loving population through a journey of perceiving brass music in a different way, especially for the high school student like myself. Prior to the video, we listened to and regarded the Canadian Brass almost as figures of high deity—Gods of the Brass World! You have produced a video which makes brass playing look relatively achievable… I truly regard the Canadian Brass as an institution of music all on its own, and have much admiration and gratefulness of your work and message to the youth of the Brass World.

Dear Sirs,

I am an avid fan of the Canadian Brass. Being a high school student and trumpet player I have come to love the Brass as most young people my age love rock stars. I have sixteen of their recordings, the Live video, and posters in my bedroom and locker...

For some reason, Chuck tends to get more mail from young players than anyone else in the group. The following is a common example:

Dear Mr. Daellenbach,

I am a junior in high school and I am a real big fan of the Canadian Brass. The members...are phenomenal along with the pieces of musc that they play. I play tuba and I think you are awesome...

Many times letters are written to inquire about the availability of the music played by the Brass. For the reader's information, all Canadian Brass published music is available from Hal Leonard Publishing, and may be ordered through any music store.

Perhaps the most satisfying and touching letters are those from young players who have been inspired enough by the Brass' example to start a brass ensemble of their own.

Dear Canadian Brass,

I am a high school student. As a trumpet player, I was introduced to your group several years ago...I have truly fallen in love with your music, and formed a brass quintet for our fifth annual Christmas concert.

Dear Canadian Brass,

My brother, his friend, my friend, and I have a brass quartet. We call ourselves the Brass Bandits... We play music from all eras including the 20s, 30s, traditional, patriotic, Christmas and a little John Williams. I have included six Brass Bandits cards. With the first five, I would like you to each autograph one and have them sent back to me. The sixth is for you to keep. Thank you very much.

But you can't please everybody, and there is that rare letter...

> Dear Canadian Brass,
>
> ...I hope people of other countries do not think you are typical Canadian musicians. It would be better if you moved to New Orleans.

And then there is *this* letter...

> Dear Sirs,
>
> Send me please one copy of your accordion and organ catalogue. Thank you very much.

DISCOGRAPHY

As of 6/1/92. Organized by recording label, with year of release, or projected release. All titles are in print and may be ordered from any retailer.

Philips Classics

BOURBON STREET 1993
All arrangements by Luther Henderson.

Bourbon Street (Traditional), Ballin' the Jack, Bill Bailey (Cannon), Black Bottom Stomp (Morton), Goin' Home (Henderson), Jelly and the Vamp (Henderson), King Porter Stomp (Morton), Kitten on the Keys (Comfrey), Lonely Boy Blues (Morton), Maple Leaf Rag (Henderson), Melancholy Baby, Nearer My God to Thee, Shoe Shiner's Drag (Morton), The Entertainer (Joplin), The Pearls (Morton), The Wolverines (Morton), Twelfth Street Rag, You Made Me Love You

THE WAGNER ALBUM 1992
All titles by Richard Wagner; all transcriptions by Arthur Frackenpohl.

Ride of the Walküries from *Die Walküre*, Funeral March from *Götterdämmerung*, Dance and Entry from *Die Meistersinger*, Entry of the Guests from *Tannhäuser*, Pilgrims' Chorus from *Tannhäuser*, Overture to *Rienzi*, Prelude to Act III of *Lohengrin*, Bridal Chorus from *Lohengrin*, Prelude to Act III from *Die Meistersinger*, Elsa's Procession to the Cathedral from *Lohengrin*, Prelude to *Tristan und Isolde*, The Evening Star from *Tannhäuser*, Träume (no. 5 from the "Wesendonck" Lieder)

THE ESSENTIAL CANADIAN BRASS (432 571-2) 1992

Zarathustra Fanfare (R. Strauss/Mills), Concerto for Two Trumpets in C (Vivaldi/Mills), Canzone prima a 5 (Gabrielli/McNeff), Turkish Rondo (Mozart/Frackenpohl), "Little" Fugue in G Minor (Bach/Romm), Beale Street Blues (Handy/Henderson), Largo al factotum (Rossini/Kulesha), Theme, Interludes and Re-variations from Serenade K. 361 (Mozart/Henderson), The Flight of the Tuba Bee (Rimsky-Korsakov/Cable), La

Virgen de la Macarena (arr. Romm), Cannon Song from Threepenny Opera (Weill/McNeff), Amazing Grace (arr. Henderson), Tuba Tiger Rag (arr. Henderson), Toccata and Fugue in D Minor (Bach/Mills), The Well-Tampered Bach (arr. Henderson), Canon (Pachelbel/Mills), The Saints' Hallelujah (arr. Henderson)

RED, WHITE AND BRASS: MADE IN AMERICA 1991
With members of the Boston Symphony and the New York Philharmonic; Lukas Foss, conductor.

Voluntary on Old One-Hundredth (arr. Wright), American Patrol (arr. Norris), George M. Cohan on Broadway (arr. Wright), Westward Ho (arr. Wright), A Salute to John Philip Sousa (arr. Wright), Alexander's Ragtime Band (Berlin/Wright), Grand Circus Fantasia (arr. Wright), Shaker Suite (arr. Wright), Beautiful Dreamer (Foster/Henderson)

BEETHOVEN: SYMPHONY NO. 5 (426 487-2) 1991
With members of the Boston Symphony and the New York Philharmonic; Georg Tintner, conductor.

Egmont Overture (trans. Frackenpohl), Symphony No. 5 in C Minor, complete (trans. Frackenpohl), Wellington's Victory or the Battle of Vittoria (trans. McNeff)

THE CHRISTMAS ALBUM (426 835-2) 1990
With the Festival Singers of Canada, directed by Elmer Iseler.

Carol of the Bells (arr. McNeff), Away in a Manger (arr. McNeff), Jingle Bells (arr. McNeff), The First Nowell (arr. McNeff), Dance of the Sugar Plum Fairy (Tchaikovsky/McNeff), We Three Kings (arr. McNeff), Angels from the Realms of Glory (arr. McNeff), Coventry Carol (arr. McNeff), C'ou viens-tu, bergere (arr. Cable), The Twelve Days of Christmas (arr. Cable), O Come Immanuel (arr. Gillis), I Wonder as I Wander (arr. Gillis), What Child Is This (arr. Gillis), La Cloche de Noel (arr. Cable), We Wish You a Merry Christmas (arr. McNeff), Noël Nouvelet (arr. Cable), Hark! the Herald Angels Sing (arr. McNeff), Silent Night (arr. McNeff), Good King Wenceslas (arr. McNeff), Hallelujah Chorus from *Messiah* (Handel/Mills), Lo, How a Rose E'er Blooming (arr. Cable), O Come, All Ye Faithful (arr. McNeff)

Sony Classics (formerly CBS Masterworks)

CANADIAN BRASS: ENGLISH RENAISSANCE MUSIC
(MK45792) 1990

The Bells (Byrd/Kroll), Callino Casturame (Byrd/Kroll), Fortune (Byrd/
Kroll), Pavan of Five Parts (Dering/Kroll), The Silver Swan (Gibbons/
Kroll), The Honeysuckle (Holborne/Kroll/Alman), Coranto: Heigh Ho
Holiday (Holborne/Kroll), Galliard (Holborne/Kroll), Lullaby
(Holburne/Kroll), Thus Bonny Boots (Holmes/Kroll), Doe You Not
Know (Morley/Kroll), My Bonnie Lass (Morley/Kroll), O Care Thou
Wilst Despatch Me (Weelkes/Kroll), The Lady Oriana (Wilbye/Kroll),
Oft Have I Vowed (Wilbye/Kroll), The Satyr's Dance (Johnson/Cable),
Rowland—Lord Willoughby's March (Byrd/Cable), Coranto
(Bull/Cable), The Fitzwilliam Suite (Byrd/Cable), The Woods So Wil
(Byrd/Frackenpohl), Alman (Byrd/Frackenpohl), Favana (Byrd/
Frackenpohl), Galiarda (Byrd/Frackenpohl), La Volta (Byrd/
Frackenpohl), The Earle of Oxford's Marche (Byrd/Frackenpohl)

THE MOZART ALBUM (MK-44545) 1989
Transcription by Arthur Frackenpohl.

Overture to *The Magic Flute*, Sarastro's Aria "O Isis und Osiris" from *The
Magic Flute*, Queen of the Night's Aria from *The Magic Flute*, Tuba Mirum
from the Requiem, Alleluia from Exultate Jubilate, Ave Verum Corpus,
Figaro's Aria "Non più andrai" from *The Marriage of Figaro*, Rondo alla
Turca, Adagio & Fugue K. 546, Theme & 5 Variations K. 501, Adagio &
Allegro K. 594

THE BEST OF CANADIAN BRASS (MK 45744) 1989

Deus in Adjutorium (Monteverdi/Frackenpohl), Canzon V
(Gabrieli/Frackenpohl), Canon in D (Pachelbel/Frackenpohl), Overture
to *The Marriage of Figaro* (Mozart/Bergler), Non più andrai from *The
Marriage of Figaro* (Mozart/Mills), Ave verum corpus (Mozart/Watkin),
Queen of the Night's Vengeance Aria from *The Magic Flute*
(Mozart/Cable), Alleluia from *Exultate, jubilate* (Mozart/Mills), Rondo
Alla Turca (Mozart/Frackenpohl), from "The Four Seasons:"
Spring—first movement (Vivaldi/ Frackenpohl), Summer—third
movement (Vivaldi/Frackenpohl), Autumn—third movement
(Vivaldi/Frackenpohl), Winter—second movement
(Vivaldi/Frackenpohl); Contrapunctus I from *The Art of the Fugue* (Bach),
Contrapunctus VIII from *The Art of the Fugue* (Bach), Contracpunctus
XIII (rectus) from *The Art of the Fugue* (Bach), Basin Street Blues

(Williams/Henderson), Chinatown, My Chinatown
(Jerome/Henderson), Just a Closer Walk with Thee (arr. Gillis), The
Saints' Hallelujah (Handel/Henderson)

GABRIELI/MONTEVERDI: ANTIPHONAL MUSIC 1989
*Featuring Principal Brass of the New York Philharmonic and the Boston
Symphony Orchestra. Kazuyoshi Akiyama, conductor. Transcriptions by
Arthur Frackenpohl.*

Monteverdi: Vespers of the Blessed Virgin (1610), Christmas Vespers.
Gabrieli: Canzon per sonare No. 1 "La Spiritata," Canzon per sonare No.
2, Canzon per sonare No. 3, Canzon per sonare No. 4, Canzon in Double
Echo, Canzon quarti toni (a 15), Canzon II, Canzon V, Canzon VI,
Canzon X, Canzon XII, Canzon XIV, Canzon XVI

BACH: THE ART OF THE FUGUE (MK-44501) 1988
Transcription by Arthur Frackenpohl.

The entire work, Contrapunctae I-XIV, ending with the chorale prelude
on "Vor deinem Thron tret ich hiermit."

BASIN STREET (FM-42367) 1987
With George Segal, banjo and vocals. All arrangements by Luther Henderson.

Sweet Georgia Brown, Amazing Grace, St. Louis Blues, Muskrat Ramble,
The Sheik of Araby, Beale Street Blues, Strummin' with George, Basin
Street Blues, Glory Look Away, South Rampart Street Parade, Royal
Garden Blues, High Society March, St. James Infirmary, Chinatown,
That's a Plenty, Bill Bailey

VIVALDI: THE FOUR SEASONS (MK-42095) 1986
Transcription by Arthur Frackenpohl.

Contains the complete set of four concertos: Spring (La Primavera),
Summer (L'Estate), Autumn (L'Autumno), Winter (L'Inverno)

A CANADIAN BRASS CHRISTMAS (FM-39740) 1985
Arranged by Luther Henderson.

Bring a Torch, Jeanette, Isabella, The Christmas Song, Ding Dong
Merrily on High, Frosty the Snow Man, Go Tell it on the Mountain, God
Rest Ye Merry Gentlemen, Good Christian Men Rejoice, Have Yourself a
Merry Little Christmas, Here We Come a-Wassailing, I Saw Three Ships,
The Little Drummer Boy, Rudolph the Red Nosed Reindeer, Silver Bells,
Sussex Carol, White Christmas, Winter Wonderland

BRASS IN BERLIN (IM-39035) 1984
Double Quintets with the Berlin Philharmonic Brass.

Canon (J. Pachelbel), Magnificat (C.T. Pachelbel), Echo Song (Lassus), In nomine (Gibbons), Jesu meine Freude (Bach), Singet dem Herrn ein neues Lied (Bach), Jubilate Deo (Gabrieli), Sonata pian' e forte (Gabrieli), In ecclesiis (Gabrieli), Sonata XIII (Gabrieli), Adagio (Albinoni), Jubilate Deo (Palestrina)

CANADIAN BRASS LIVE (M-39515) 1984
Recorded at the National Arts Centre in Ottawa.

Just a Closer Walk with Thee (arr. Gillis), Overture to *The Marriage of Figaro* (Mozart), Canzona per sonare No. 4 (Gabrieli), Excerpts from"The Four Seasons" (Vivaldi), The Dog-Gone Blues (Henderson), Tuba Tiger Rag (arr. Henderson), Pete Meets the Beat (Henderson), Kanon (Pachelbel), Tribute tot he Ballet, The Saints' Hallelujah (arr. Henderson), Boy Mozart (Kompanek)

CHAMPIONS (FM-37797) 1983

Winner's Circle (Kompanek), Honky Cat (Elton John), C'etait Toi (Billy Joel), Scarborough Fair, Maxwell's Silver Hammer (Lennon-McCartney), Fantasy (M. White-Del Barrio-V. White), We Are the Champions (Mercury), Living for the City (Stevie Wonder), A Bit of Whimsey (Gillis), A Whiter Shade of Pale (Reid-Brooker), Video Brass (Gillis)

RCA/BMG Red Seal

CANADIAN BRASS—MORE GREATEST HITS (5628-2-RC) 1988

Sabre Dance (Khachaturian), Largo al factotum from *The Barber of Seville* (Rossini), La Cumparsita (Rodriguez), Carmen Suite (Bizet): Overture/Seguidilla/Habañera/Toreador Song, Little Fugue in G Minor (Bach), Wachet auf ruft uns die stimme (Bach), Galliard Battaglia (Scheidt), Prelude and Fugue on the Name BACH (Bach), Girl with the Flaxen Hair (Debussy), Golliwogg's Cakewalk (Debussy), Minstrels (Debussy), The Rhythm Series (Gershwin): Clap Yo' Hands/Fidgety Feet/Fascinating Rhythm/I Got Rhythm, A Foggy Day/Nice Work If You Can Get It (Gershwin), Bess You Is My Woman Now (Gershwin), Just a Closer Walk with Thee (arr. Gillis), Adagio (Barber), Shreveport Stomp(Morton), Alligator Crawl (Waller), Carolina Shout (Johnson), Tuba Polka (Clarinet Polka)

STRIKE UP THE BAND (6490-4-RC) 1987
All titles by George Gershwin, arranged by Luther Henderson.

Strike Up the Band, Someone to Watch Over Me, The Rhythm Series
(Medley): Clap Yo' Hands/Fidgety Feet/Fascinating Rhythm/I Got
Rhythm, A Foggy Day/Nice Work If You Can Get It, The Man I Love,
Rialto Ripples, Three Preludes for Piano, *Porgy and Bess* Suite:
Introduction/Jasbo Brown Blues/Summertime, It Ain't Necessarily So,
Bess You Is My Woman Now, I Loves You Porgy, A Woman Is a
Sometime Thing/I Got Plenty o' Nuttin', Oh Lawd I'm on My Way

CANADIAN BRASS GREATEST HITS (ARL1-4733) 1983

A Sousa Collection (arr. Cable), Allegro Maestoso from "Water Music"
(Handel), Canon (Pachelbel/Mills), Carnival of Venice (Staigers/Eaton),
Fanfare "Albason" (Reiche), Grandpa's Spells (Jelly Roll Morton),
Hallelujah Chorus (Handel), Handful of Keys (Waller), Loungin' at the
Waldorf (Waller), Rondeau, theme from "Masterpiece Theatre" (Mouret),
Toccata and Fugue in D Minor (Bach), Trumpet Voluntary (Purcell)

HIGH, BRIGHT, LIGHT AND CLEAR: THE GLORY OF BAROQUE
BRASS (ARC1-4574) 1982

Brandenburg Suite No. 1 (Bach), Air on the G String (Bach), Fanfare
"Albason" (Reiche), Galliard Battaglia (Scheidt), Praeludium und Fuge
über den Namen BACH (Bach), Prince of Denmark March (Clarke),
Purcell Suite (Purcell), Rondeau, theme from "Masterpiece Theatre"
(Mouret), William Boyce Suite

CHRISTMAS WITH THE CANADIAN BRASS (ARL1-4733) 1981

Angels from the Realms of Glory, Angels We Have Heard on High,
Away in a Manger, Coventry Carol, Deck the Hall, The First Nowell,
Good King Wenceslas, Hallelujah Chorus (Handel), Hark! the Herald
Angels Sing, The Holly and the Ivy, Jingle Bells, O Come Emmanuel/I
Wonder as I Wander, O Christmas Tree, O Come All Ye Faithful/Joy to
the World, O Holy Night, O Little Town of Bethlehem/It Came Upon a
Midnight Clear, Silent Night, What Child Is This

PACHELBEL CANON AND OTHER GREAT BAROQUE HITS
(ARL1-3554) 1980

Canon (Pachelbel/Mills), "Gigue Fugue" in G Major (Bach), Little Fugue in G Minor (Bach), Passacaglia and Fugue in C Major (Bach), Sheep May Safely Graze (Bach), Suite from "Water Music" (Handel), Toccata (Frescobaldi), Toccata and Fugue in D Minor (Bach), Wachet auf ruft uns die Stimme (Bach)

THE VILLAGE BAND (ATC1-3924) 1980

Largo al factotum from *The Barber of Seville* (Rossini), Sempre libera from *La Traviata* (Verdi), A Sousa Collection (arr. Cable), A Stephen Foster Treasury (arr. Cable), Carnival of Venice (Staigers/Eaton), Poet and Peasant Overture (von Suppe), Flight of the Tuba Bee (Rimsky-Korsakov), The War Between the States (Cable)

AIN'T MISBEHAVIN' (ARL1-5030) 1979
Titles by Fats Waller unless otherwise noted. The album was originally titled "Mostly Fats."

Ain't Misbehavin', Alligator Crawl, Black and Blue, Carolina Shout (J.P. Johnson), Grandpa's Spells (Jelly Roll Morton), Handful of Keys, I've Got a Feelin' I'm Fallin', Jitterbug Waltz, Just a Closer Walk with Thee (traditional, arr. Gillis), Lookin' Good But Feelin' Bad, Loungin' at the Waldorf, Mean to Me (Turk/Ahlert), Sherveport Stomp (Jelly Roll Morton), Spreading Rhythm Around (McHugh/Koehler)

Vanguard Records

CANADIAN BRASS (VCD-72018)
This collection includes all the material previously released on two Boot Records titles, "Canadian Brass: Pachelbel to Joplin" (1973) and "Canadian Brass in Paris" (1974).

Toccata and Fugue in D Minor (Bach), Songs of Newfoundland (Cable), Just a Closer Walk with Thee (arr. Gillis), Sonata for Trumpet and Organ (Purcell), Fugue in G Minor (Bach), A Diversion (Symonds), Air pour les Trompettes (Bach), Sonata in Three Movements (Purcell), Kanon (Pachelbel), Staggering (McCauley), Madrigal (Schein), Golyardes' Grounde (Forsythe), Renaissance Suite: In Pride of May (Weelkes), Aria (Fux), Gigue; Music for Brass Instruments in Three Movements: Chorale Fantasy, Intermezzo, Fugue (Dahl); Hallelujah Chorus (Handel)

CBC Enterprises

CANADIAN BRASS ENCORE (MVCD1011)
This collection includes material previously released on the albums entitled "Rag-Ma-Tazz" (1974) and "Unexplored Territory" (1977) both from CBC.

Canadian Brass Rag (Rathburn), The Cathedral (Bach), A Royal Firework (Handel), Golliwog's Cakewalk (Debussy), Days Before Yesterday (Crosley), En Sueño (Gillis), First Gymnopedie (Satie), The Joust (Gillis), Entertainer Rag (Joplin), Ragtime Waltz (Joplin), Sycamore Rag (Joplin) Euphonic Sounds Rag (Joplin), Rosebud March (Joplin), Figleaf Rag (Joplin), Easy Winners Rag (Joplin), 'Lasses Trombone (Fillmore), Slim Trombone (Fillmore), Amazing Grace, Bourbon Street Medley: Just a Closer Walk with Thee, Tin Roof Blues, Muskrat Ramble

V I D E O G R A P Y

All available on VHS (titles with asterisks are also available in the PAL format); distributed by Hal Leonard Publishing.

STRINGS, WINDS, AND ALL THAT BRASS:
THE INSPIRATION OF MUSIC (50481640) 1992
Color, stereo, 20 minutes

The Canadian Brass interviews students about the experience of making music and playing in bands, orchestras and ensembles. The production is designed as an inspirational tool for motivating students, and informational to parents of prospective instrumental players. Features a guest appearance by Wynton Marsalis, and players from the New York Philharmonic and the Boston Symphony.

CANADIAN BRASS ON STAGE AT WOLF TRAP (50481394) 1991 *
Color, stereo, 56 minutes

A live concert at Wolf Trap, America's National Park for the Performing Arts, featuring special guest Judith Blegen, star of the Metropolitan Opera. Music of Bach, Gershwin, Gabrieli, Rossini, Dixieland, and "Gilda and the 5 Dukes," a send-up of Verdi's *Rigoletto*. Also includes the cowboy "opera for brass" *Hornsmoke*, by P.D.Q. Bach (Peter Schickele).

THE CANADIAN BRASS MASTER CLASS (50488557) 1989 *
Color, stereo, 55 minutes

The Brass works with students, illustrating points of playing and performing. In 4 sections: A video essay about the Canadian Brass, Posture and Breathing, Tonguing and Embouchure, and Music Performance and Playing with an Ensemble. Released in cooperation with Music Educators National Conference.

THE CANADIAN BRASS SPECTACULAR (50488569) 1989
Color, stereo, 60 minutes
With members of the Boston Symphony and the New York Philharmonic. Georg Tintner, conductor.

A live concert, featuring Beethoven's Fifth Symphony (first movement only), Wellington's Victory (Beethoven), Variations on a Theme of Thomas Tallis (Vaughan Williams), Salute to John Philip Sousa, Beale Street Blues, and music by Gabrieli and Monteverdi.

CANADIAN BRASS LIVE (50488559) 1986 *
Color, stereo, 50 minutes

The quintet in concert, recorded live. A Red Ribbon winner in the American Film and Video Association Awards. Includes Just a Closer Walk, The Saints' Hallelujah, Carnival of Venice, Handful of Keys, Canzona per sonare No. 4 (Gabrieli), Little Fugue in G Minor (Bach), Boy Mozart, Tribute to the Ballet.

THE CANADIAN BRASS
MUSIC LIBRARY

All are published through Hal Leonard Publishing, and may be ordered from any music retailer.

CANADIAN BRASS EDUCATIONAL SERIES

CANADIAN BRASS BOOK OF BEGINNING QUINTETS
with exercises and techniques
arranged and edited by Walter Barnes

Music from the Royal Fireworks (Handel), Ode to Joy (Beethoven), Sanctus (Schubert), Saint Anthony (Haydn), Amazing Grace (American), Westminster Abbey (Purcell), Steal Away (Spiritual), Echo Carol (Christmas), A la Clair Fontaine (French), Processional (German), Crimond (Scottish), Chorale (Bach), Tudor Motet (Tye), Kelligrew's Soiree (Canadian), Fanfare for a Maple Leaf (Canadian), Battle Hymn of the Republic (American)

50396780 Trumpet I in B flat, 50396790 Trumpet II in B flat, 50396820 Horn in F, 50396800 Trombone, 50396810 Tuba, 50396770 Conductor, 50396760 Cassette of Canadian Brass performing the collection

CANADIAN BRASS BOOK OF EASY QUINTETS
with discussion and techniques
arranged and edited by Walter Barnes

Hosanna (Palestrina), Non Nobis Domine (Byrd), The Silver Swan (Gibbons), Intrada—A Fanfare (Pezel), Fugue in E flat (Bach), Air from "Water Music" (Handel), Ave Verum (Mozart), Ave Maria (Rachmaninoff), Cwn Rhondda (Welsh), Carol of the Bells (Ukrainian), El Yivneh Hagalil (Israeli), Bones (Spiritual), Three Newfoundland Folksongs (Canadian), The Lord Bless You and Keep You (Lutkin), My Country 'Tis of Thee, O Canada (Lavalee)

50396060 Trumpet I in B flat, 50396070 Trumpet II in B flat, 50396040 Horn in F, 50396050 Trombone, 50396080 Tuba, 50396090 Conductor, 50396720 Cassette of Canadian Brass performing the collection

CANADIAN BRASS BOOK OF FAVORITE QUINTETS
(Intermediate Level)
with discussion and techniques
arranged and edited by Walter Barnes

Trumpet Voluntary (Clarke), Trumpet Tune and Ayre (Purcell), Canon
(Pachelbel), Rondeau (Mouret), Largo (Handel), Hallelujah Chorus
(Handel), My Heart Ever Faithful (Bach), Contrapunctus I (Bach),
Andante from Trumpet Concerto (Haydn), Cor Royal
(Nicoali/Cornelius), Sakura & Kimigayo (Japanese), Farandole (Bizet),
Toreador Song (Bizet), Hava Nagila (Israeli), Just a Closer Walk
(American/arr. Gillis), Amazing Grace (American/arr. Henderson)

50488966 Trumpet I in B flat, 50488967 Trumpet II in B flat, 50488968
Horn in F, 50488969 Trombone, 50488970 Tuba, 50488971 Conductor,
50488972 Cassette of Canadian Brass performing the collection

CANADIAN BRASS BOOK OF ADVANCED QUINTETS
with discussion and techniques
arranged and edited by Walter Barnes

Trumpet Voluntary (Stanley), Three Elizabethan Madrigals (Morley,
Dowland), Hosanna to the Son of David (Gibbons), Antiphonal
(Sweelinck), Hallelujah, Amen (Handel), Where'er You Walk (Handel),
We Hasten with Eager Footsteps (Bach), Fantasia and Fugue (Bach),
Gloria from *Lord Nelson Mass* (Haydn), Grand March from Aida (Verdi),
Jerusalem (Parry), Gaudeamus Igitur (Collegium Musicum), Three
Spirituals (arr. Barnes), Overture to *HMS Pinafore* (Sullivan)

50480314 Trumpet I in B flat, 50480315 Trumpet II in B flat, 50480316
Horn in F, 50480317 Trombone, 50480318 Tuba, 50480319 Conductor,
50480320 Cassette of Canadian Brass performing the collection

CANADIAN BRASS SERIES OF COLLECTED QUINTETS

EASY CLASSICS
arranged by Charles Sayre

Two Chorales: O Sacred Head/Break forth O beauteous heavenly light
(Bach), Two Fuguing Tunes: When Jesus Wept/Kittery (Billings),
Victorious Love (Amor Vittorioso) (Gastoldi), In the Hall of the
Mountain King (Grieg), Austrian Hymn (Haydn), Canon (Tallis)

50488760 Trumpet I in B flat, 50488761 Trumpet II in B flat, 50488762

Horn in F, 50488763 Trombone, 50488764 Tuba, 50488765 Conductor.

HYMNS FOR BRASS (easy level)
arranged by Rick Walters

Ah Holy Jesus, Beautiful Savior, Christ the Lord is Risen Today, Eternal
Father Strong to Save, A Mighty Fortress, We Gather Together

50488754 Trumpet I in B flat, 50488755 Trumpet II in B flat, 50488756
Horn in F, 50488757 Trombone, 50488758 Tuba, 50488759 Conductor.

RODGERS AND HAMMERSTEIN HITS (easy level)
arranged by Charles Sayre

Edelweiss from *The Sound of Music*, Oklahoma from *Oklahoma!*, You'll
Never Walk Alone from *Carousel*, Oh What a Beautiful Mornin' from
Oklahoma!, Blow High, Blow Low from *Carousel*, Honey Bun from *South
Pacific*.

50488766 Trumpet I in B flat, 50488767 Trumpet II in B flat, 50488768
Horn in F, 50488769 Trombone, 50488770 Tuba, 50488771 Conductor.

BRASS ON BROADWAY (intermediate level)
arranged by Bob Lowden

Broadway Baby from *Follies*, Comedy Tonight from *A Funny Thing
Happened on the Way to the Forum*, Get Me to the Church on Time from
My Fair Lady, Ol' Man River from *Show Boat*, Sunrise, Sunset from
Fiddler on the Roof, They Call the Wind Maria from *Paint Your Wagon*.

50488778 Trumpet I in B flat, 50488779 Trumpet II in B flat, 50488780
Horn in F, 50488781 Trombone, 50488782 Tuba, 50488783 Conductor.

FAVORITE CLASSICS (intermediate level)
arranged by Henry Charles Smith

Gavotte from Sixth Cello Suite (Bach), Prayer from *Hansel and Gretel*
(Humperdinck), Cantate Domino (Pitoni), The Liberty Bell (Sousa),
Questo e' quella from *Rigoletto* (Verdi), Pilgrim's Chorus from
Tannhäuser (Wagner).

50488784 Trumpet I in B flat, 50488785 Trumpet II in B flat, 50488786
Horn in F, 50488787 Trombone, 50488788 Tuba, 50488789 Conductor.

IMMORTAL FOLKSONGS (intermediate level)
arranged by Terry Vosbein

Greensleeves, High Barbary, Londonderry Air, Shenandoah, Simple Gifts, The Drunken Sailor

50488772 Trumpet I in B flat, 50488773 Trumpet II in B flat, 50488774 Horn in F, 50488775 Trombone, 50488776 Tuba, 50488777 Conductor.

CANADIAN BRASS LIMITED EDITIONS

Material commercially recorded and performed in concert.

BACH: THE ART OF THE FUGUE (complete) (50488553)
transcribed for brass quintet by Arthur Frackenpohl

MONTEVERDI: VESPERS TO THE BLESSED VIRGIN (1610) (50488554)
transcribed for triple brass quintet by Arthur Frackenpohl

MUSSORGSKY: PICTURES AT AN EXHIBITION (50488555)
transcribed for brass quintet by Arthur Frackenpohl

TRIBUTE TO THE BALLET (50488562)
arranged for brass quintet by Sonny Kompanek

VIVALDI: THE FOUR SEASONS (complete) (50488556)
transcribed for brass quintet by Arthur Frackenpohl

CANADIAN BRASS ENSEMBLE SERIES

Material commercially recorded and performed in concert; all are brass quintets.

A CANADIAN BRASS CHRISTMAS
arranged by Luther Henderson, with optional keyboard/synthesizer accompaniment

Bring a Torch, Jeanette, Isabella; Ding Dong Merrily on High; Go Tell it on the Mountain; God Rest Ye Merry Gentlemen; Here We Come a-Wassailing; The Huron Carol; I Saw Three Ships; Sussex Carol.

50489973 Trumpet I in B flat, 50489974 Trumpet II in B flat, 50489975 Horn in F, 50489976 Trombone, 50489977 Tuba, 50489978 Keyboard, 50489979 Conductor

Individual titles in the Ensemble series; set of parts and score.

ADAGIO ("Adagio for Strings")— Barber/McNeff 50488458
AIN'T MISBEHAVIN' — Waller/Norris 50396380
AIR ON THE G STRING — Bach/Frackenpohl 50396680
ALL BREATHING LIFE — Bach/Smith 50488730
AMAZING GRACE — arr. Henderson 50488791
ART OF THE FUGUE SUITE
    (Contrapunctae I, IX, VII)—Bach/Frackenpohl 50488460
BILL BAILEY —Cannon/Henderson 50488457
BRANDENBURG SUITE I —Bach/Frackenpohl 50396390
BRANDENBURG SUITE II — Bach/Frackenpohl 50507150
CANADIAN BRASS RAG —Rathburn 50488752
CANZONE PER SONARE NO. 4 —Gabrieli/Page 50396400
CARMEN SUITE NO. 1 — Bizet/Mills 50488603
CAROL OF THE BELLS — Leontovich/Frackenpohl 50507200
CONCERTO —Vivaldi-Bach/Baldwin 50396710
COVENTRY CAROL — arr. Gillis, with organ 50489338
DOG GONE BLUES, THE —Henderson 50507120
ELEVEN CHORALE PRELUDES —Brahms/Sauer 50507130
FIRST NOWELL, THE — arr. Cable, with organ 50396360
FLIGHT OF THE TUBA BEE —Rimsky-Korsakov/Cable 50396660
A FOGGY DAY/NICE WORK IF YOU CAN GET IT
    —Gershwin/Henderson 50488462
FUGUE IN G MINOR ("LITTLE") — Bach/Romm 50488401
GALLIARD BATTAGLIA —Scheidt 50396370
GIRL WITH THE FLAXEN HAIR — Debussy/Kulesha 50489587
GLORY, LOOK AWAY (Dixie/Battle Hymn) — arr. Henderson 50488402
GOLYARDES' GROUNDE —Forsyth 50488733
GOOD KING WENCESLAS —arr. Gillis, with organ 50396200
GYPSY RONDO — Haydn/Frackenpohl 50396340
HALLELUJAH CHORUS —Handel/Mills (quintet alone) 50488751
HALLELUJAH CHORUS —Handel/Mills, with organ 50507180
HANDFUL OF KEYS —Waller/Henderson 50396290
HARK! THE HERALD ANGELS SING — arr. Frackenpohl, with organ
    50396300
HILLS OF ANACAPRI, THE —Debussy/Kulesha 50489588
HOLLY AND THE IVY, THE —arr. Cable 50396110
IN DULCI JUBILO — arr. Frackenpohl, with organ 50489340
INTERMEZZO, OP. 117, NO. 1 — Brahms/Gaylord 50507350
JIG FUGUE IN G MAJOR — Bach/Sauer 50396350
JINGLE BELLS — arr. Cable, with organ 50396120
JOPLIN CONCERT SUITE — Joplin/Daellenbach-Mills 50488731
JUST A CLOSER WALK WITH THEE — arr. Gillis 50396690

KANON — Pachelbel/Mills 50488734
KILLER TANGO — Kompanek 50396750
LA CUMPARSITA —Rodriguez/Kompanek 50396670
LARGO AL FACTOTUM from *The Barber of Seville* —Rossini/Kulesha
    50396320
MARRIAGE OF FIGARO OVERTURE —Mozart/Bergler 50507140
MINSTRELS —Debussy/Kulesha 50489589
NEWFOUNDLAND SKETCH —arr. Cable 50396330
NOMADIC FIVE — Rathburn 50489341
O COME ALL YE FAITHFUL/JOY TO THE WORLD
    —arr. Cable, with organ 50396130
O COME EMMANUEL/I WONDER AS I WANDER
    —arr Gillis, with organ 50489342
O HOLY NIGHT — Adam/Frackenpohl 50489343
O ISIS UND OSIRIS —Mozart/Frackenpohl 50507090
O LITTLE TOWN OF BETHLEHEM/IT CAME UPON A MIDNIGHT
    CLEAR —arr. Cable, with organ 50507210
PASSACAGLIA AND FUGUE IN C MINOR — Bach/Balm 50396250
PERPETUAL MOTION —J. Strauss/Cable 50396260
PETE MEETS THE BEAT —Henderson 50480321
PIRATES OF PENZANCE — Sullivan/Watkin 50502820
POET AND PEASANT OVERTURE — von Suppé/Mills 50396270
PORGY AND BESS SUITE —Gershwin/Henderson 50488461
PRAELUDIUM UND FUGE UBER DEN NAMEN "BACH"
    — Bach/Mills 50396280
PRINCE OF DENMARK'S MARCH — Clarke/Mills 50396230
PURCELL SUITE — Purcell/Mills 50396240
RONDEAU Theme from Masterpiece Theatre—Mouret/Mills 50396700
SAINTS' HALLELUJAH (When the Saints Go Marching In/Hallelujah
    Chorus) — Henderson 50488459
SARABANDE — Handel/Robertson 50480324
SHEEP MAY SAFELY GRAZE — Bach/Watts 50396170
SILENT NIGHT —arr. Frackenpohl, with organ 50489346
SONATA FOR 2 TRUMPETS AND BRASS — Purcell/Mills 50488753
SOUSA COLLECTION — Sousa/Cable 50480323
SUITE FROM WATER MUSIC —Handel/Mills 50396730
TOCCATA AND FUGUE IN D MINOR — Bach/Mills 50396210
TUBA TIGER RAG — arr. Henderson 50507110
TURKISH MARCH — Beethoven/Frackenpohl 50396160
TURKISH RONDO — Mozart/Frackenpohl 50396150
WAR BETWEEN THE STATES 1861-1865 — Cable 50480322
WESTMINSTER CAROL — arr. Gillis, with organ 50507190
WHAT CHILD IS THIS — arr. Gillis, with organ 50396140
WILLIAM BOYCE SUITE — Boyce/Cable 50396190

DOUBLE BRASS QUINTETS

ADAGIO IN G MINOR — Albinoni-Giazotto/Mills 50396840
CANON — Pachelbel/Frackenpohl 50396850
ECHO SONG —Di Lasso/Frackenpohl 50396860
IN ECCLESIIS — Gabrieli/Fawcett 50396830
IN NOMINE — Gibbons/Frackenpohl 50396870
JESU, JOY OF MAN'S DESIRING — Bach/Mills 50396740
JUBILATE DEO — Gabrieli/Frackenpohl 50396880
JUBILATE DEO — Palestrina/Frackenpohl 50396890
MAGNIFICAT — Pachelbel/Frackenpohl 50396900
SING YE TO THE LORD — Bach/Frackenpohl 50396910
SONATA XIII — Gabrieli/Frackenpohl 50396930
SONATA PIANO E FORTE — Gabrieli/Frackenpohl 50396920

CANADIAN BRASS CONCERT BAND SERIES

Signature quintet arrangements transcribed for band; complete set of score and parts.

A CANADIAN BRASS CHRISTMAS — arr. Cable 08721378
A CANADIAN BRASS CHRISTMAS SUITE — arr. Custer 04050318
BEALE STREET BLUES — Handy/Marshall 08724006
JUST A CLOSER WALK WITH THEE — Gillis/Custer 08721094
LA VIRGEN DE LA MACARENA — trans. Custer 08724008
SAINTS' HALLELUJAH — Henderson/Custer 08721323
SOUSA COLLECTION — Cable 08721374
SUITE FROM WATER MUSIC — Handel/Custer 08721325

THE CANADIAN BRASS
COLLECTION OF INSTRUMENTS

At the beginning of 1991 the Canadian Brass began a new venture into the instrument business. Inspired by their years of friendship and collaboration with Renold Schilke, the Brass formed Canadian Brass Enterprises in the pursuit of a mutual dream—marketing a special line of brass instruments, hand-crafted to their specifications. Whereas performers usually have unique, customized instruments not available to the public, the Brass have made the exact instruments that they play on stage available to a worldwide market. When asked why the venture was initiated, Chuck responded, "Certain manufacturers' instruments would have elements of the sound qualities we wanted for own performances and recordings, but no one instrument had everything. We have designed the instruments of The Canadian Brass Collections to deliver maximum flexibility, allowing the professional brass player and advanced student to play the widest range of musical styles without having to maintain an array of alternate instruments for different musical requirements."

The instruments of the Canadian Brass Collection:

Trumpets & Cornets

Yellow Brass, .460" bore, 5 1/6" soldered rim bell, hand-lapped monel pistons, hand-lapped slide tubes.

CB 10 B-flat Trumpet
CB 11 C Trumpet
CB 14 B-flat Cornet
CB 15 E-flat Cornet
CB 17 B-flat/A Piccolo Trumpet

French Horns

Yellow brass; .465" bore, 10 1/4" bell, single piece, one seam formed Kruspe style bell, Geyer-style valve arrangement with ball joint valve mechanisms.

CB 40 Fixed bell model double Horn in F/B-flat
CB 41 Detachable-bell model double Horn in F/B-flat

Trombones

Yellow brass, .547" (13.89) bore; 8 1/2" bell, hand-lapped slide tubes, red brass bell.

CB 20 Tenor Trombone with F attachment
CB 21 Tenor Trombone

Tubas

Yellow brass, .689" bore, 19 1/4" bell, front action valves, compact 4-quarter size tuba.

CB 50 CC Tuba
CB 51 BB-flat Tuba

Speech made at Honorary Doctor of Music degree presentation
New England Conservatory of Music
May 15, 1992

Since its founding in 1867, New England Conservatory of Music has bestowed only 123 honorary doctor of music degrees. This is the first time that an ensemble is so honored. The occurrence is unique because the ensemble is unique.

The Canadian Brass is not only an assemblage of master musicians, it is also an entity with a creative life of its own. Since being formed in 1970, the Brass has rescued the brass quintet from a role on the fringes of music, with few historical models, little credibility among classical musicians, and almost no available repertory. Composers seek out opportunities to write for them. Critics acclaim them. The world's riches adhere to them. The Canadian Brass has almost singlehandedly generated this sea-change of opinion, taste and opportunity.

In their own words, their role is not to bring music to the audience, but to bring the audience to music. That their music is so accessible—indeed is so much *fun* that one cannot resist it—owes much to their showmanship and love of entertainment. They have not feared to take the classicism out of classical music, and they have gleefully knocked the starch out of the stiff and self-important composure of classical musicianship. It is no stretch to say that they have changed forever the relationship of classical musicians to their audience, and audiences around the world have loved them for it. The number of people reached by and touched by their performances and recordings is in the incalculable millions.

But let no one think that they are less than serious about music. These performers are consummate masters of their instruments, and they have set new standards of style and virtuosity. Critics have noted them for "ensemble playing of remarkable unanimity."

Their playing has also led a whole generation of kids—in high school and even younger—to aspire to a new level. And the Brass has never abandoned their role in education. They have consistently found time in their schedules for youth, whether high school assemblies for the uninitiated, masterclasses with serious young musicians, or new ventures into the unchartered realm of instruction via video. This afternoon they conducted a master-workshop for Conservatory students and teenagers alike.

New England Conservatory's founder, Eben Tourjée, was an entrepreneur. He believed in making waves. Each of the members of the Canadian Brass is educated in the classical master-apprentice tradition, which New England Conservatory embodies. What they have learned would make Tourjée proud. They have taken from their education not classical norms, but individual creativity. They have etched their own way.

Not only do the members of the Canadian Brass play 24-carat-gold matched instruments, they are 24-carat-gold matched musicians.